D0116241

Franco & Friends

FOOD FROM THE WALNUT TREE

Buon Appetito
Francesco Taruschio

Franco & Friends

FOOD FROM THE WALNUT TREE

ANN & FRANCO TARUSCHIO

Photography by Jean Cazals

BBC BOOKS

This book is published to accompany the television series
Franco & Friends – Food from the Walnut Tree which was made for
BBC Wales by Prospect Pictures.
Producer: Mark John

© Prospect / Ann & Franco Taruschio 1997
Ann and Franco Taruschio have asserted their right to be
identified as the authors of this work in accordance with the
Copyright Designs and Patents Act 1996

The recipes on pages 27 and 140, Lady Llanover's Salt Duck
with Pickled Damsons and Whimberry Sorbet, are taken from
Leaves from The Walnut Tree by Ann & Franco Taruschio,
published by Pavilion in 1993, and are reproduced by kind
permission of Pavilion Books Ltd.

Photographs © BBC Worldwide
Home economist: Marie-Auge Lapierre
Stylist: Antonia Gaunt
Designed by Ann Burnham
Drawings by Andrew Farmer

ISBN 0 563 38376 3

First published in 1997 by BBC Books,
an imprint of BBC Worldwide Ltd,
80 Wood Lane, London W12 0TT

Reprinted 1997

Colour separations by Radstock Reproductions Ltd,
Midsomer Norton
Printed in Great Britain by Cambus Litho Ltd, East Kilbride
Bound in Great Britain by Hunter & Foulis Ltd, Edinburgh
Jacket printed by Lawrence Allen Ltd, Weston-super-Mare

CONTENTS

INTRODUCTION

First of all, let me tell you a little about myself. I am an Italian living in Wales. My formative years were spent in the Marche, an area little known by the British, which is half way down Italy on the east coast. The Adriatic laps its coast line, and the Apennine hills and the Sibillini mountains are in the interior. It is an area of spectacular views.

When I married a British girl in 1963, we opened a restaurant, The Walnut Tree Inn, near Abergavenny in the Marches of Wales, an area not dissimilar to where I hail from in Italy. The restaurant is to be found in the rural parish of Llanddewi Skirrid, tucked under the Skirrid Mountain, otherwise known as the Holy Mountain. The rivers Gavenny and Usk flow through the town and the Black Mountains rise to the north east. I quickly felt at home with the area.

It is from the surrounding mountains, meadows and rivers that many of the ingredients for our recipes come: Welsh lamb from the lowlands and mountains, as well as an abundance of game; wild salmon and trout from the rivers; whimberries from the hills; and fresh porcini and girolles from the woods. Local Italian market gardeners still supply us with fruit and vegetables.

It was a different story in our early days. I remember that I wanted to prepare one of the traditional dishes of the Marche, *Brodetto*, a stew of mixed fish and shellfish in a rich wine- and tomato-based sauce. I needed a good supply of fresh fish, but just couldn't get it. Abundant fish are found off the coast of Wales, but at that time, in the early 60s, it was all either sent to Billingsgate in London or boats from France collected it and took it back for the French market. Very little fish stayed in Wales. It took time for us to make contacts in Solva, Milford Haven, Llanstephan and Swansea. As the fishermen's trust in us grew, so our supplies became easier.

And *Brodetto* rapidly became one of the signature dishes at The Walnut Tree. Eventually Penclawdd and Crofty supplied us with laver seaweed, laverbread, cockles and samphire.

Another traditional dish of the Marche is *Porchetta*, a whole young pig stuffed with rosemary and wild fennel and then roasted. Local farmers had to be convinced to supply us with the right size pig. It took a bit of persuading. Lamb was never a problem to obtain because we are surrounded by sheep farmers. In fact, many farmers export their sheep to Italy, especially young lamb to be made into *Abbacchio*, which is whole young lamb cooked with wine, garlic and rosemary.

I am still preparing dishes that have been cooked in the Marche for hundreds of years, dishes that have a culture and history behind them. Italian food has deep roots in the country's history. Where did the idea of peasant food come from? In the Marche, peasant and Count eat the same dishes; there is no distinction. In Italy, it is not a question of class who eats what. It is a question of everyone having a love for food. Eating in Italy is almost a religious rite. Many dishes are only eaten on or during certain religious festivals, of which there are many.

The Welsh recipes I have incorporated into my repertoire also fit into a historical framework. Lady Llanover's salt duck has now become another signature dish at The Walnut Tree. Lady Llanover was a great exponent of Welsh cooking during the late nineteenth century. Her cookery book is a classic.

In some of our recipes I have blended the two cultures, of Wales and Italy — Roasted Monkfish with Laverbread Sauce and Fried Seaweed is one example, Spaghetti and Penclawdd Cockle Sauce is another. It is surprising how similarities crop up when comparing the two countries' cuisines. In Wales a popular dish is baked trout wrapped with bacon; in Italy we find baked trout wrapped in pancetta or speck, but given the fillip of a little savory or sage tucked inside.

Part of the pleasure of cooking in rural Wales is that one becomes personally involved with the produce. It is not a question of buying it from a shop or wholesaler, prepacked and soulless. Here we have close contact with our suppliers or we can gather or collect produce ourselves. The lady who supplies us with venison comes from one of the oldest estates in the area. The venison is wild and the woodlands where the deer roam are hundreds of years old. When I make *Bresaola* (traditionally cured beef) from venison it gives me great pleasure to translate an Italian dish by using Welsh produce.

In the Autumn months, if it's a good season, fresh porcini abound in Wales. The Welsh have never really bothered with collecting them, but the Italians and East Europeans, who have settled in Wales, are out with their baskets, rushing to their well-guarded secret patches. We have a little network of mushroom collectors now. It is unbelievable how jealous and secretive mushroom collectors can become. They always behave as though they have been on an MI5 mission. I shall never forget the night two very tired ladies turned up with a van full, literally chock-a-block, with porcini. The ladies had picked all day and then had driven from West Wales to deliver them to us.

A very popular dish on our menu is *Vincisgrassi*, an eighteenth-century baked pasta dish from the Marche. It is made from layers of pasta, locally collected porcini, truffles, prosciutto and a rich béchamel.

To know that the recipes from both Italy and Wales that I use are being used by other chefs and personal cooks makes me very happy. I feel I am sharing a little of the culture of my country of birth and my country of adoption.

FT

ANTIPASTI

SARDE ANCONETANE
GRATIN OF SARDINES WITH ROSEMARY

SERVES **4–6**

These sardines are prepared in the style of the Adriatic port of Ancona, in the Marche region. Ancona, which comes from the Ancient Greek word Ankon *meaning elbow, is the only town in Italy where you can see the sun both rising from and setting in the sea.*

500G (1LB 2OZ) FRESH
SARDINES, CLEANED, SCALED
AND BONED, TAIL LEFT ON
55G (2OZ) FRESH BREADCRUMBS
I SPRIG FRESH ROSEMARY,
FINELY CHOPPED

For the sauce
2 TABLESPOONS EXTRA
VIRGIN OLIVE OIL
I SMALL ONION, FINELY CHOPPED
I WINEGLASS DRY WHITE WINE
300G (10½ OZ) TOMATOES,
SKINNED, SEEDED AND CRUSHED
SALT AND FRESHLY
GROUND BLACK PEPPER

To make the sauce, heat the oil in a saucepan and fry the onion until soft and translucent. Add the wine and boil until it has almost all evaporated. Add the tomato pulp and season with salt and pepper. Reduce the sauce until it is thick.

Preheat the oven to 180°C/350°F/gas 4. Put the sauce in a round terracotta gratin dish. Place the sardines on top, opened up like a book, skin side down. Fan the sardines, tail end to the edge of the dish. Mix together the breadcrumbs and rosemary, and season with salt and pepper. Sprinkle over the sardines.

Bake the gratin for 20 minutes. Serve hot.

Frittelle di Salvia e Acciughe
Sage and anchovy fritters

SERVES **4**

The best time to make this recipe is May and June, when sage leaves are tender and have a delicate flavour.

Rinse the sage leaves and dry thoroughly. Drain the anchovy fillets of excess oil on kitchen paper.

Break the egg into a bowl and beat lightly. Add the flour, wine and oil. Mix all the ingredients together thoroughly until smooth, then leave this batter to rest for one hour.

Line up half of the sage leaves on the work surface. Put an anchovy fillet on each leaf, cover with another sage leaf and secure with a wooden cocktail stick.

Heat abundant light olive oil in a frying pan. Dip the anchovy and sage 'packets' in the batter and drop into the hot oil. Fry until golden brown on both sides. Drain on kitchen paper. Serve hot with aperitifs or as part of an antipasto.

24 LARGE FRESH SAGE LEAVES

12 ANCHOVY FILLETS
 PRESERVED IN OIL

1 EGG

150G (5½OZ) PLAIN FLOUR

2–3 TABLESPOONS WHITE WINE

1 TABLESPOON OLIVE OIL

OLIVE OIL FOR DEEP FRYING

Crostini con Formaggio Pecorino
Crostini with fresh pecorino

SERVES **4**

The highly scented white truffle – tartufo bianco – is much prized by Italians. Truffle oil gives a hint of its distinctive aroma. St Angelo in Vado, in the Marche, is famous for its truffles.

Preheat the grill. Toast the bread lightly under the grill. Put the slices of pecorino on top and sprinkle with the Parma ham. Return the crostini to the grill and grill until the cheese is melted. Drizzle with truffle oil and serve at once.

4 SLICES BAGUETTE OR CIABATTA

200G (7OZ) FRESH PECORINO,
 CUT IN 5MM (¼IN) SLICES

30G (1OZ) PARMA HAM, CUT
 IN JULIENNE

TRUFFLE OIL

CROSTINI MEDITERRANEI

CROSTINI WITH AUBERGINE, TOMATO AND CHILLI

*Crostini are thin slices of bread that are toasted, preferably
on a griddle so that they are lightly charred, and then topped with
all manner of savoury ingredients – sausage, vegetables,
cheese, seafood and so on.*

Heat half the oil in a frying pan and fry the spring onions,
garlic, oregano, marjoram and chilli briefly, stirring with
a wooden spoon. Add the red pepper and cook for 10
minutes, adding a little water to moisten the mixture. Add the
tomatoes and season with salt and pepper. Continue cooking
for 5 minutes.

In another frying pan, heat the remaining oil and fry the
aubergine for 5 minutes, stirring. Season with salt and
pepper. Add the tomato and pepper mixture to the aubergine
and cook 5 more minutes. Stir in the basil.

Toast the bread, on both sides, on a griddle or ridged cast-
iron grill pan. Distribute the vegetable mixture among the
crostini, piling it up on top. Serve.

4 TABLESPOONS EXTRA
  VIRGIN OLIVE OIL
4 SPRING ONIONS,
  FINELY CHOPPED
1 CLOVE GARLIC, CRUSHED
A PINCH OF DRIED OREGANO
A PINCH OF DRIED MARJORAM
½ SMALL CHILLI,
  FINELY CHOPPED
100G (3½OZ) RED PEPPER,
  FINELY DICED
250G (9OZ) TOMATOES, SKINNED,
  SEEDED AND DICED
100G (3½OZ) AUBERGINE,
  FINELY DICED
10 FRESH BASIL LEAVES, TORN
8 SLICES BAGUETTE OR CIABATTA,
  ABOUT 1CM (½IN) THICK
SALT AND FRESHLY
  GROUND BLACK PEPPER

RIGHT *Crostini Mediterranei*

GLAMORGAN SAUSAGES

These are a Welsh speciality — delicious meatless sausages made with hard white cheese and breadcrumbs generously flavoured with herbs and mustard, coated with crumbs and deep fried.
To make a Welsh-style 'fritto misto', *serve them with* Porri al Prosciutto Impanati e Fritti *and cockle fritters (see page 124).*

550G (1¼LB) CAERPHILLY
  CHEESE, GRATED
450G (1LB) DAY-OLD
  WHITE BREADCRUMBS
8 TABLESPOONS FINELY
  CHOPPED SPRING ONIONS
5 EGGS, SEPARATED
4 HEAPED TABLESPOONS FINELY
  CHOPPED PARSLEY
2 TEASPOONS FRESH
  THYME LEAVES
4 LEVEL TEASPOONS ENGLISH
  MUSTARD POWDER
SALT AND FRESHLY
  GROUND BLACK PEPPER
PLAIN FLOUR
FINE DRY BREADCRUMBS
OIL FOR DEEP FRYING

Mix together the cheese, day-old breadcrumbs, spring onions, egg yolks, parsley, thyme, mustard, salt and pepper. Shape into sausages the size of a little finger. Dip the sausages first in flour to coat lightly and then in the lightly beaten egg whites, then roll in dry breadcrumbs. Refrigerate for 30 minutes.

Deep fry the sausages in light oil until golden brown all over. Drain on kitchen paper and serve at once.

CROCCHÉ DI PATATE SICILIANE
SICILIAN POTATO CROQUETTES

SERVES 6

This recipe originates in Palermo, Sicily, where both crocché *and* panelle *(see page 150) are sold by* friggitore *from stalls on street corners.*

Cook the potatoes in boiling salted water, or in a microwave oven. When the potatoes are cool enough to handle, peel them, then put through the middle grade disc of a mouli-légumes or a potato ricer. Do not use a food processor, as it would make the potatoes gluey. Add the butter, parsley, mint, Parmesan and a seasoning of salt. Add the 3 egg yolks and mix in well.

Oil your hands, and shape the potato mixture into balls the size of a large thumb. Dip the *crocchette* first in flour to coat lightly and then in the egg whites beaten with the whole egg, then roll in breadcrumbs. Fry the *crocchette* in abundant hot olive oil until they are golden brown all over. Drain on kitchen paper and serve at once.

1.2KG (2¾LB) POTATOES

50G (1¾OZ) BUTTER, DICED

2 TABLESPOONS FINELY CHOPPED PARSLEY

2 TABLESPOONS FINELY CHOPPED FRESH MINT

5 TABLESPOONS FRESHLY GRATED PARMESAN

SALT

4 EGGS, 3 OF THEM SEPARATED

PLAIN FLOUR

FINE DRY BREADCRUMBS

OLIVE OIL FOR DEEP FRYING

Cozze al Pesto di Trapani

GRILLED MUSSELS WITH TOMATOES, ALMONDS AND FENNEL

SERVES 4

This mussel dish originates from Trapani in Sicily — a town famous for salt. The dish is often served in the Marche.

Scrub the mussels well, and remove any beards. Discard mussels that have cracked shells or open shells that do not close when tapped. Put the cleaned mussels in a large pan set over a very high heat. Cook, shaking the pan occasionally, until the shells open. Discard the empty shells, keeping the mussels on their half shells. Also discard any mussels that remain stubbornly closed.

Put the bread cubes, garlic and almonds in a food processor and process until fine. Add this mixture to the tomatoes and fennel, and season with salt and pepper.

Preheat the grill. Arrange the mussels, on their half shells, on a baking tray. Put a little of the tomato and almond mixture on each mussel, covering it well. Sprinkle with a little olive oil and place under the grill for a few minutes until golden brown and crisp. Serve hot.

1.5KG (3¼LB) MUSSELS
2 SLICES BREAD, CRUSTS REMOVED, DICED AND FRIED IN OLIVE OIL UNTIL GOLDEN BROWN
1 CLOVE GARLIC, PEELED
30G (1OZ) BLANCHED ALMONDS, TOASTED
500G (1LB 2OZ) PLUM TOMATOES, SKINNED, SEEDED AND FINELY DICED
1 BUNCH OF HERB FENNEL FRONDS, PREFERABLY WILD, FINELY CHOPPED
EXTRA VIRGIN OLIVE OIL
SALT AND FRESHLY GROUND BLACK PEPPER

RIGHT *Cozze al Pesto di Trapani*

CROCCHETTE DI RICOTTA
RICOTTA AND PARMESAN CROQUETTES

SERVES **4**

Serve these with Insalata di Radicchio al Parmigiano e all'Aceto Balsamico *(see page 22).*

300G (10½OZ) RICOTTA

100G (3½OZ) PARMESAN, FRESHLY GRATED

15G (½OZ) PLAIN FLOUR

2 EGGS

1 TABLESPOON FINELY CHOPPED FRESH CHIVES

SALT AND FRESHLY GROUND BLACK PEPPER

FINE DRY BREADCRUMBS

5 TABLESPOONS EXTRA VIRGIN OLIVE OIL

Sieve the ricotta into a bowl. Add the Parmesan, flour, eggs, chives and a seasoning of salt and pepper. Amalgamate together well. The mixture should be fairly firm. Shape into croquettes, 7cm (2¾in) long and 3cm (1¼in) wide, and roll in breadcrumbs.

Heat the olive oil in a frying pan and fry the croquettes until golden on all sides. Remove from the oil with a perforated spoon and drain on kitchen paper. Serve hot.

BRUSCHETTE MARINATE
BRUSCHETTA WITH MARINATED RED MULLET

SERVES **4**

1 SMALL ONION, FINELY CHOPPED

5 TABLESPOONS EXTRA VIRGIN OLIVE OIL

4 RED MULLET FILLETS, WEIGHING 400G (14OZ) IN TOTAL, SKIN SCALED

½ WINEGLASS DRY WHITE WINE

SALT AND FRESHLY GROUND BLACK PEPPER

4 RIPE TOMATOES, SKINNED, SEEDED AND CUT IN JULIENNE

JUICE OF 1 LEMON

2 TABLESPOONS CHOPPED PARSLEY

4 SLICES PUGLIESE-TYPE BREAD

1 CLOVE GARLIC, PEELED

Fry the onion in 2 tablespoons of the olive oil until golden brown. Add the red mullet fillets and briefly fry, then add the wine. Cook until the wine has reduced by half. Season with salt and pepper. Cover the pan, remove from the heat and leave to cool until tepid.

Remove the mullet fillets from the pan to a dish. Filter the cooking juices and drizzle 3 tablespoons over the fish. Scatter the tomatoes over and sprinkle with the lemon juice, remaining olive oil, parsley and pepper to taste. Leave to marinate for 30 minutes.

Toast the slices of bread on both sides (ideally on a griddle or ridged cast-iron grill pan), then rub with the garlic; discard the garlic. Place a mullet fillet on top of each slice of bread and spoon the marinade over. Serve at once.

Tortini di Funghi e Melanzane

LAYERED PORCINI, AUBERGINE AND SCAMORZA MOULDS

SERVES **6**

Scamorza is a firm, fresh, delicately flavoured cheese from Campania, usually made from cow's milk but also sometimes from goat's or buffalo's milk. It is similar to mozzarella, which can be substituted if scamorza is not available.

450G (1LB) AUBERGINES
EXTRA VIRGIN OLIVE OIL
SALT AND FRESHLY
  GROUND BLACK PEPPER
350G (12OZ) FRESH PORCINI
  MUSHROOMS, CUT INTO STRIPS
BUTTER
FRESH SAGE LEAVES
FRESH ROSEMARY
100G (3½OZ) SCAMORZA,
  SLICED

Cut the unpeeled aubergines crossways into very thin slices. Sprinkle the slices with a little olive oil and season with salt and pepper. Grill the slices on a ridged cast-iron grill pan or griddle until tender, turning once.

Sauté the porcini strips in hot oil and butter with a few leaves of sage and a sprig of rosemary. In another pan, melt some butter with a few leaves of sage, then set aside in a warm place to infuse.

Preheat the oven to 180°C/350°F/gas 4. Oil 6 crème caramel moulds or ramekins. Layer the aubergines, porcini and scamorza in the moulds, beginning and ending with aubergine. Bake for 7 minutes. Remove from the moulds and serve hot, with a little hot sage-flavoured butter spooned over the top.

GAMBERI CROCCANTI

TIGER PRAWNS IN A CRISP PASTA CRUST

SERVES 4

Campofilone maccheroncini is a very special dried fine noodle made in Campofilone, which is in the Marche region. You can find this pasta in the UK, in Italian delicatessens.

Cook the maccheroncini in boiling water for 1 minute, just to soften it, then drain and rinse under cold running water. Drain again and put on a clean cloth to dry.

Peel the prawns. Season with salt and pepper, then wrap each one loosely in maccheroncini. Heat abundant olive oil in a deep frying pan. Fry the pasta-wrapped prawns, a few at a time, until golden all over. Remove the prawns with a slotted spoon and drain on kitchen paper. Keep warm.

Make a dressing by mixing together the balsamic vinegar, olive oil and spring onions. Put a spoonful of the dressing in the centre of each plate, place the prawns on top and add a wedge of lemon. Serve immediately.

25G (SCANT 1OZ) CAMPOFILONE
  MACCHERONCINI
400G (14OZ) RAW TIGER PRAWNS
SALT AND FRESHLY
  GROUND BLACK PEPPER
OLIVE OIL FOR DEEP FRYING
4 LEMON WEDGES
For the dressing
4 TABLESPOONS BALSAMIC
  VINEGAR
4 TABLESPOONS EXTRA
  VIRGIN OLIVE OIL
4 MEDIUM SPRING ONIONS,
  CHOPPED INTO THIN RINGS,
  GREEN INCLUDED

RIGHT *Gamberi Croccanti*

POLPETTINE DI RICOTTA E SPINACI

RICOTTA AND SPINACH BALLS

MAKES **20**

These polpettine *are good served as part of a hot vegetarian antipasto, or just eaten on their own.*

Roughly chop the spinach. Sieve the ricotta into a bowl and add the spinach to it. Add the Parmesan, 1 egg, the fresh breadcrumbs, nutmeg and salt to taste. Amalgamate well. Divide into 20 equal portions and shape each into a ball.

Beat the remaining egg with the milk and a pinch of salt. Lightly coat the ricotta balls in flour and then in the egg mixture, then roll in dry breadcrumbs. Deep fry in abundant hot olive oil until golden brown all over. Drain on kitchen paper and serve at once.

450G (1LB) COOKED SPINACH, WELL DRAINED

450G (1LB) RICOTTA

60G (2OZ) PARMESAN, FRESHLY GRATED

2 EGGS

2 TABLESPOONS FRESH BREADCRUMBS

A PINCH OF FRESHLY GRATED NUTMEG

SALT

4 TABLESPOONS MILK

PLAIN FLOUR

FINE DRY BREADCRUMBS

OLIVE OIL FOR DEEP FRYING

INSALATA DI RADICCHIO AL PARMIGIANO E ALL'ACETO BALSAMICO

RADICCHIO AND PARMESAN SALAD WITH BALSAMIC VINEGAR

SERVES **4**

Serve this with Crocchette di Ricotta *(see page 18).*

Cut each well-washed radicchio lengthways into 4 and dry thoroughly. Dress with the oil, vinegar, and a seasoning of salt and pepper, making sure the leaves are well coated. Put the radicchio into a serving dish. With a potato peeler or truffle shaver, shave the Parmesan on top.

2 SMALL HEADS RADICCHIO

3 TABLESPOONS EXTRA VIRGIN OLIVE OIL

2 TABLESPOONS BALSAMIC VINEGAR

SALT AND FRESHLY GROUND BLACK PEPPER

50G (1¾OZ) PARMESAN

Insalata di Patate alla Rucola
New potato and rocket salad

SERVES 6

For this simple salad, a good extra virgin olive oil is needed, one that is dense and strong in flavour. In the Marche we buy our oil directly from the frantoio, *the olive oil press.*

B ring a pan of salted water to the boil. Add the potatoes and a drop of vinegar and cook for about 12 minutes or until tender. Drain. Leave the potatoes to get cold.

Cut the potatoes into 3 or 4, depending on the size, then toss them with the rocket, olives, anchovies, tomatoes and olive oil. Leave the potatoes to marinate for at least 1 hour. Before serving, season with salt, pepper and a drop of vinegar.

1.2KG (2¾LB) NEW POTATOES

WHITE WINE VINEGAR

1 BUNCH OF ROCKET,
  FINELY CHOPPED

12 BLACK OLIVES, STONED
  AND CHOPPED

6 ANCHOVY FILLETS PRESERVED
  IN OIL, DRAINED AND CHOPPED

150G (5½OZ) PLUM TOMATOES,
  SKINNED, SEEDED AND CUT INTO
  SMALL DICE

150ML (¼PINT) EXTRA
  VIRGIN OLIVE OIL

SALT AND FRESHLY GROUND
  BLACK PEPPER

Fritto alla Garisenda
Fried parma ham, parmesan and truffle sandwiches

MAKES 10

C ut a 7cm (2¾in) disc from the centre of each slice of bread. Cut the Parma ham to fit 10 of the discs, and cover with the Parmesan shavings. Spread the truffle paste on the remaining bread discs. Make sandwiches by covering the Parma ham and Parmesan discs with the truffle paste discs, paste side down. Press each sandwich lightly with your hand so that the edges of the discs stick together.

Dip each sandwich in cold milk and then in beaten eggs, then coat with breadcrumbs. Make sure the breadcrumbs cover the sandwiches evenly and adhere well.

Heat abundant olive oil in a frying pan and fry the sandwiches until golden on both sides. Drain on kitchen paper, and serve at once.

20 THIN SLICES BREAD

100G (3½OZ) PARMA HAM, SLICED

80G (SCANT 3OZ) PARMESAN CHEESE,
  SHAVED

50G (1¾OZ) WHITE
  TRUFFLE PASTE

COLD MILK

4 EGGS, LIGHTLY BEATEN

50G (1¾OZ) FINE DRY
  BREADCRUMBS

LIGHT OLIVE OIL FOR DEEP FRYING

Tortini di Patate alla Mozzarella e Pomodoro

POTATO CAKES TOPPED WITH MOZZARELLA AND TOMATO

SERVES 4

This is a quick, easy and nourishing dish to make for vegetarians.

To make the potato *pizze*, cook the potatoes, in their skins, in boiling salted water for 20–25 minutes or until tender. (When cooking old potatoes, put them into cold salted water, bring the water to the boil and then reduce the heat so that the water just simmers.) Drain well. When the potatoes are cool enough to handle, peel them. Pass the warm potatoes through a potato ricer or mouli-légumes to make a fine purée. Add the whole egg, egg yolks, flour, melted butter, parsley, salt and pepper to the potato purée and mix well. Divide the mixture into 4 and shape each portion into a flat disc or *pizza* about 15cm (6in) in diameter.

Heat 1 tablespoon of olive oil with a knob of butter in a small frying pan just large enough to accommodate the *pizza* (or in a larger pan that will hold 2 *pizze* at a time). Add one of the potato *pizze* and cook over a low heat, without turning, for 5 minutes. Distribute one quarter of the mozzarella slices over the *pizza*, followed by one-quarter of the tomato slices, slightly overlapping, in the centre. Dot with a few olive slices, and add a pinch each of salt, pepper and oregano. Sprinkle with a little olive oil. Continue cooking, covered, for a further 10 minutes. Prepare the other 3 *tortini* in the same way. Serve hot, sprinkled with small basil leaves.

EXTRA VIRGIN OLIVE OIL

BUTTER

150G (5½OZ) MOZZARELLA, THINLY SLICED

3 PLUM TOMATOES, SKINNED AND SLICED

8 BLACK OLIVES, STONED AND SLICED

DRIED OREGANO

FRESH BASIL LEAVES, TO GARNISH

For the potato 'pizze'

700G (1LB 9OZ) OLD POTATOES

1 EGG PLUS 2 EGG YOLKS

100G (3½OZ) PLAIN FLOUR

30G (1OZ) BUTTER, MELTED

2 TABLESPOONS FINELY CHOPPED PARSLEY

SALT AND FRESHLY GROUND BLACK PEPPER

RIGHT *Tortini di Patate alla Mozzarella e Pomodoro*

Torta di Aglio Selvatico e Ricotta

WILD GARLIC AND RICOTTA TART

SERVES 8

Wild garlic, or ramsons, with its fresh green leaves and pretty white flowers, is a common sight in damp woods. It is very easy to grow in the garden. The garlic flavour is quite strong. Roman and Greek soldiers ate garlic to increase strength and aggression – or so they believed!

For the filling

200G (7OZ) WILD GARLIC LEAVES

2 TABLESPOONS OLIVE OIL

A PINCH OF GROUND CHILLI

1 TEASPOON FINELY CHOPPED
GARLIC

SALT AND FRESHLY
GROUND BLACK PEPPER

225G (8OZ) RICOTTA

3 EGGS, LIGHTLY BEATEN

60G (2OZ) PARMESAN, FRESHLY
GRATED

6 TABLESPOONS DOUBLE CREAM

FRESHLY GRATED NUTMEG
TO TASTE

For the pastry

225G (8OZ) PLAIN FLOUR

A PINCH OF SALT

1 LEVEL TABLESPOON ICING SUGAR

150G (5½OZ) SOFTENED
BUTTER

1 EGG, BEATEN

To make the pastry, sift the flour, salt and sugar into a bowl and lightly rub in the butter until the mixture resembles breadcrumbs. Add the egg and sprinkle over a few drops of chilled water. Work in lightly with your fingertips to bind to a dough. Leave the dough to rest in the refrigerator for 1 hour.

Preheat the oven to 220°C/425°F/gas 7. Roll out the pastry dough and line a 25cm (10in) loose-bottomed flan tin. Prick the bottom of the pastry case with a fork, and bake blind for about 15 minutes. Allow to cool.

Turn the oven down to 180°C/350°F/gas 4.

Blanch the wild garlic in boiling water for a few minutes if young and tender (or 10 minutes if the garlic is older), then drain and roughly chop. Heat the oil in a frying pan, add the wild garlic and toss for a few minutes. Season with the chilli, chopped garlic, salt and pepper, and remove from the heat. Add the ricotta, beaten eggs, Parmesan, double cream and nutmeg to taste. Mix in well. Spread the mixture in the pastry case. Bake for 30 minutes or until the pastry is browned and the filling set.

Lady Llanover's Salt Duck with Pickled Damsons

SERVES 6

For this dish use only the breast of duck, left on the bone. Serve the duck breast thinly sliced with gooseberry pickle, crab apple and rowanberry jelly and pickled damsons.

DUCK BREASTS

COARSE SEA SALT

For the pickled damsons

4 LITRES (7 PINTS) DAMSONS

1.8KG (4LB) PRESERVING SUGAR

450ML (¾ PINT) RED WINE
  VINEGAR

1 X 10CM (4IN) STICK CINNAMON

6 CLOVES

Weigh the duck breasts and for every 2.7kg (6lb) of duck meat and carcass allow 225g (8oz) of coarse sea salt. Rub the salt into the duck. Place the duck in a deep container, breast side down, and keep in a cool place. After 1½ days turn the breasts over. After 3 days rinse off the salt.

Preheat the oven to 150°C/300°F/gas 2. Place the duck breasts in a deep baking dish set in a baking tray. Cover the duck with cold water and also put water in the baking tray. Place in the centre of the oven and cook, uncovered, for 1½ hours. Remove the duck breasts from the liquid and leave to cool.

To prepare the pickled damsons, prick the fruit with a silver fork. Make a syrup from the sugar and vinegar. Put the damsons in the syrup and bring the syrup back to the boil. Remove the damsons at this point, using a perforated spoon, and lay them on flat trays to cool quickly. Add the spices to the syrup and boil for a further 5–10 minutes or until the syrup thickens again. Put the fruit carefully into sterilized glass jars and strain the syrup over the fruit while it is still hot. Cover while still hot. Keeping time? Until next crop.

Carpaccio di Pesce Pescatrice

Carpaccio of monkfish

SERVES 4

The best capers come from Pantelleria, an island off the coast of Italy, which is known as the black pearl of the Mediterranean. The plants grow on rocky terrain and have small, delicate orchid-like flowers which one rarely sees, as capers are the flower buds. The smaller the caper, the better the quality. Caper fruits occur when the plant has been allowed to flower. Only use very fresh monkfish for this dish.

Deep fry the capers in hot olive oil until they are crisp (they look like little flowers when deep-fried). Drain on kitchen paper.

Bone the monkfish tail and trim it well, removing the grey membrane that covers the flesh. Cut each monkfish fillet across into very thin slices.

Put a veil of olive oil on the plates. Slice the monkfish very thinly and place on the plates. Season with salt, pepper and a few drops of balsamic vinegar. Sprinkle the deep-fried capers over the monkfish, place the tomato dice in the centre and finish with the shredded basil scattered over.

25G (SCANT 1OZ) SALTED CAPERS, ABOUT 8 CAPERS EACH, WELL RINSED AND DRIED
OLIVE OIL FOR DEEP FRYING
500G (1LB 2OZ) MONKFISH TAIL
EXTRA VIRGIN OLIVE OIL
SALT AND FRESHLY GROUND BLACK PEPPER
BALSAMIC VINEGAR
1 PLUM TOMATO, SKINNED, SEEDED AND CUT INTO SMALL DICE
2 LARGE FRESH BASIL LEAVES, THINLY SHREDDED

RIGHT *Carpaccio di Pesce Pescatrice*

Carpaccio di Pere con Scaglie di Parmigiano e Aceto Balsamico

CARPACCIO OF PEAR AND PARMESAN WITH BALSAMIC VINEGAR

SERVES **6**

Choose a juicy, firm variety of pear for this dish.

Wash the pears, cut in half lengthways and remove the core. Slice the pears very thinly, lengthways, leaving the skin on. Put the slices of pear on 6 plates in a flower pattern. Pile the Parmesan shavings in the centre of each 'flower'. Emulsify the balsamic vinegar with the olive oil, drizzle over the pear and cheese, and serve at once.

6 RIPE PEARS

120G (4OZ) PARMESAN, SHAVED

4 TABLESPOONS BALSAMIC
  VINEGAR

8 TABLESPOONS EXTRA VIRGIN
  OLIVE OIL

Crema di Patate con Dadini di Zucca

POTATO SOUP WITH PUMPKIN AND PANCETTA

SERVES **6**

The pancetta can be omitted for vegetarians and instead the soup can be sprinkled with freshly grated Parmesan.

Melt 100g (3½oz) of the butter in a saucepan and fry the onion until golden brown. Add the potatoes and season with pepper. Reserve 4 tablespoons of the vegetable stock, and add the rest to the pan. Bring to the boil, then reduce the heat and simmer gently until the potatoes are cooked. Purée the soup in a blender and return to the saucepan. Season with salt and pepper.

While the soup is simmering, melt the remaining butter in a frying pan and add the pumpkin dice and reserved vegetable stock. Toss to coat the pumpkin with butter, then cook until the pumpkin is tender. Be careful not to overcook it or the dice will disintegrate.

Fry the pancetta in a non-stick pan, without any fat.

Reheat the potato soup if necessary, then serve with the pumpkin dice, pancetta and a sprinkling of parsley.

150G (5½OZ) BUTTER

100G (3½OZ) ONION, FINELY
  CHOPPED

500G (1LB 2OZ) POTATOES, PEELED
  AND ROUGHLY CHOPPED

SALT AND FRESHLY GROUND
  BLACK PEPPER

1 LITRE (1¾ PINTS) VEGETABLE
  STOCK (SEE PAGE 56)

300G (10½OZ) PUMPKIN FLESH,
  CUT IN SMALL DICE

6 SLICES SMOKED PANCETTA, CUT IN
  JULIENNE

1 TABLESPOON FINELY CHOPPED
  PARSLEY

ZUPPA DI FARRO
THICK SPELT AND VEGETABLE SOUP

SERVES 6

Farro *(spelt) is a very ancient and nutritious cereal, a precursor of wheat. Spelt is known in Italy as the wheat of the Romans, who made a kind of polenta from it called* puls. *The name in Italian is derived from the Latin* far, *which leads on to* farina *(flour). Spelt is cultivated mostly in central Italy where it is used for traditional dishes.*

Drain the spelt and put it in a large saucepan. Cover with fresh cold water and bring to the boil. Reduce the heat and gently simmer for 1½ hours.

At the same time, simmer the beans in another pan, in fresh water to cover, with the bay leaf, for 1½ hours. When the beans are cooked, drain them, reserving the cooking liquid. Put aside 2 cups of beans, and pass the rest through a mouli-légumes or purée in a blender or food processor.

Heat 1 tablespoon of olive oil in a saucepan and fry the onion and garlic for a few minutes. Add the carrot, celery and half the herbs and stir to mix. After a few more minutes of cooking, add the Parma ham, tomatoes, cavolo nero, the bean purée and the drained spelt. Season with the nutmeg, and salt and pepper to taste. Add the bean cooking liquid and enough vegetable stock or water to make a good thick soup consistency. Cover the pot and cook for 40 minutes. Add more stock or water, if required.

Add the reserved whole beans and the remaining herbs and olive oil, and check the salt. This soup is best if it can be left for a few hours and then reheated for serving. This will allow the spelt to absorb the flavours of the soup.

200G (7OZ) SPELT GRAIN, RINSED AND SOAKED OVERNIGHT

200G (7OZ) DRIED BORLOTTI BEANS, SOAKED OVERNIGHT AND DRAINED

I BAY LEAF

3 TABLESPOONS EXTRA VIRGIN OLIVE OIL

I ONION, FINELY CHOPPED

I CLOVE GARLIC, FINELY CHOPPED

I CARROT, FINELY DICED

I STICK CELERY, FINELY DICED

2 FRESH SAGE LEAVES, FINELY CHOPPED

NEEDLES FROM I SPRIG FRESH ROSEMARY, FINELY CHOPPED

I X 100G (3½OZ) SLICE PARMA HAM, FINELY DICED

2 PLUM TOMATOES, SKINNED, SEEDED AND DICED

100G (3½OZ) CAVOLO NERO OR SAVOY CABBAGE, FINELY SLICED

A PINCH OF FRESHLY GRATED NUTMEG

SALT AND FRESHLY GROUND BLACK PEPPER

VEGETABLE STOCK (SEE PAGE 56) OR WATER

Passatelli in Brodo di Pesce

PASSATELLI IN BROTH, WITH SOLE, RED MULLET AND SCAMPI

SERVES 8

Passatelli are 'soup strands', peculiar to the Marche and Emilia Romagna.

Skin the sole (or ask your fishmonger to do this) and remove the head; fillet the fish. Remove the scales from the red mullet, with the back of a knife or using a fish descaler. Eviscerate the mullet and remove the head; fillet the fish. Cut the sole and mullet fillets into large lozenge shapes. Peel the scampi. Set the fish and scampi aside in the fridge. Reserve the fish bones, scampi heads and shells for the broth.

Melt a large knob of butter in a large saucepan and fry the carrot, onion and celery until soft. Add the fish bones and scampi heads and shells, all well rinsed, and cook for 5 minutes. Add the thyme, marjoram, fennel seeds, saffron and chilli pepper. Pour in 2 litres (3½ pints) of water and season with salt and pepper. Bring to the boil, then reduce the heat to moderate and leave to boil gently for 1 hour. Strain the broth through a fine sieve. The broth should be clear, so do not press down on the vegetables and fish bones and shells in the sieve. Set the broth aside.

To make the *passatelli*, combine the breadcrumbs, Parmesan, flour, eggs, lemon zest, nutmeg, salt and pepper in a bowl. Mix together thoroughly, preferably by hand, for about 10 minutes. The resulting mixture will be quite a solid dough. Leave the dough in the fridge for at least 2 hours.

Put 2 ladles of the fish broth and 2 large ladles of water in a saucepan and bring to the boil. Place the dough in a potato ricer with large holes, or in a mouli-légumes with large holes, and press through, directly into the boiling liquid, to make cylinders 2.5cm (1in) long or more. Reheat the remaining broth in another saucepan, add the fish and scampi, and cook for 30-50 seconds. When the *passatelli* rise to the surface, remove them with a perforated spoon and divide them among 8 shallow soup bowls. Add the fish and scampi and ladle the boiling fish broth over. Serve at once.

For the broth

1 X 500G (1LB 2OZ) DOVER SOLE

1 X 350G (12OZ) RED MULLET

8 RAW SCAMPI (LANGOUSTINES)

BUTTER

1 CARROT, ROUGHLY CHOPPED

1 ONION, ROUGHLY CHOPPED

1 STICK CELERY, ROUGHLY CHOPPED

1 SMALL BUNCH OF FRESH THYME

1 SMALL BUNCH OF FRESH MARJORAM

A PINCH OF FENNEL SEEDS

A LARGE PINCH OF SAFFRON THREADS

A PINCH OF DRIED CHILLI FLAKES

SALT AND FRESHLY GROUND BLACK PEPPER

For the passatelli

250G (9OZ) FRESH BREADCRUMBS

120G (4OZ) PARMESAN, FRESHLY GRATED

50G (1¾OZ) PLAIN FLOUR

3 EGGS

GRATED ZEST OF 1 LEMON

A PINCH OF FRESHLY GRATED NUTMEG

SALT AND FRESHLY GROUND BLACK PEPPER

RIGHT *Passatelli in Brodo di Pesce*

ANTIPASTI

MINESTRA AFFUMICATA
SMOKED SALMON, LEEK AND RICE SOUP

SERVES **4**

This is a very simple, delicious soup. It is not made with stock, but instead relies on vegetables, herbs and wine to give flavour to the broth.

Put the leek and celery in a saucepan with 1 litre (1¾ pints) of water. Bring to the boil and simmer for 20 minutes. Season with salt and add the potatoes and a little of the parsley. Bring the soup back to the boil. Add the rice and cook for 12–13 minutes.

Add the wine to the soup and, if it seems too thick, also add a ladle of hot water. Complete the cooking of the rice, then add the smoked salmon. Check if more salt is needed and add some pepper and the remaining parsley. Serve hot.

100G (3½OZ) LEEK,
  THINLY SLICED, INCLUDING
  THE TENDER GREEN PART
50G (1¾OZ) CELERY,
  FINELY CHOPPED
SALT AND FRESHLY
  GROUND BLACK PEPPER
200G (7OZ) POTATOES, PEELED
  AND CUT IN SMALL DICE
1 BUNCH OF PARSLEY,
  FINELY CHOPPED
100G (3½OZ) ARBORIO OR OTHER
  ITALIAN RICE
100ML (3½FLOZ) DRY
  WHITE WINE
200G (7OZ) SMOKED SALMON
  TRIMMINGS, CUT IN JULIENNE

ZUPPA DI PATATE CON PORRI E AGLIO SELVATICO
LEEK AND POTATO SOUP WITH WILD GARLIC

SERVES **4**

Adding wild garlic to a leek and potato soup gives it an extra zest.

Melt the butter in a saucepan and sauté the leeks until soft. Add the potatoes and wild garlic, and season with salt and a generous amount of pepper. Pour in the boiling water. Bring to the boil, then cover the pan and reduce the heat to low. Leave the soup to simmer for 40 minutes, stirring occasionally.

Lightly mash the soup in the pan with a potato masher. The soup can be served as it is or topped with 1cm (½in) dice of bread fried in olive oil.

60G (2OZ) BUTTER
2 GOOD-SIZED LEEKS, WHITE
  PART ONLY, CUT INTO 2CM
  (¾IN) LENGTHS
450G (1 LB) POTATOES,
  ROUGHLY CHOPPED
50G (1¾OZ) WILD GARLIC
  LEAVES, WASHED AND SHREDDED
SALT AND FRESHLY
  GROUND BLACK PEPPER
1.2 LITRES (2 PINTS) BOILING
  WATER

Zuppa ai Legumi Misti e Orzo

Hearty bean and pearl barley soup with rosemary

We ate this comforting soup on a cold February day, in the southern part of the Marche, with the wind blowing off the snow-covered Apennines. The soup was served in wooden bowls, which reminded us of eating cawl, the Welsh comfort soup that also used to be served in wooden bowls and eaten with wooden spoons.

Soak all the pulses overnight. Soak the pearl barley too, but keep it separate. Drain the pulses. Heat the olive oil in a large saucepan and fry the onion, garlic and Parma ham. In another pan, heat the stock to boiling. Add the drained pulses to the prosciutto mixture (not the barley). Pour in the hot vegetable stock. Add the rosemary. Simmer the soup over a moderate heat for 1¼ hours. Add more hot stock if the soup seems to be getting very thick, but not too much because the soup should not be too liquid.

Add the drained pearl barley and the diced potatoes and cook for a further 10 minutes or until the barley and potatoes are tender. Season with salt and pepper. Remove the rosemary.

Before serving, add some garlic-infused olive oil and stir in some pecorino cheese to taste. Serve hot or cold.

40G (1½OZ) DRIED RED KIDNEY BEANS

40G (1½OZ) DRIED BORLOTTI BEANS

40G (1½OZ) DRIED WHITE SOYA BEANS OR OTHER WHITE BEANS SUCH AS HARICOT

30G (1OZ) DRIED GREEN SOYA BEANS

30G (1OZ) BROWN LENTILS

30G (1 OZ) DRIED WHOLE PEAS

30G (1OZ) DRIED CHICKPEAS

40G (1½OZ) DRIED BUTTER BEANS

90G (3OZ) PEARL BARLEY

3 TABLESPOONS EXTRA VIRGIN OLIVE OIL

100G (3½OZ) ONION, FINELY CHOPPED

2 CLOVES GARLIC, FINELY CHOPPED

70G (2½OZ) PARMA HAM, FINELY CHOPPED

2 LITRES (3½PINTS) STRONG VEGETABLE STOCK (SEE PAGE 56)

2 SPRIGS FRESH ROSEMARY

3 MEDIUM POTATOES, DICED

SALT AND FRESHLY GROUND BLACK PEPPER

EXTRA VIRGIN OLIVE OIL INFUSED WITH GARLIC

FRESHLY GRATED PECORINO

Passata di Ceci con Scampi

Smooth chickpea soup with scampi

SERVES **4**

This delicious soup comes from the province of Pesaro. It can also be made with fava beans instead of chickpeas and scallops instead of scampi. Crostini of bread toasted in the oven is often eaten with it.

Fry the scampi in the olive oil with the garlic and parsley until the scampi are almost cooked. Add the wine and cook for another minute or so or until the scampi are opaque. Remove the scampi and peel them, then return them to the pan. Remove from the heat and keep warm.

Purée the chickpeas in a blender with some of their cooking liquid. The resulting *passata* should be quite dense and smooth. Season with salt. Reheat the *passata* and pour into bowls. Add the scampi with their cooking liquid. Serve with extra virgin olive oil and freshly ground black pepper.

400G (14OZ) FRESH SCAMPI
  (LANGOUSTINES), IN SHELL
4 TABLESPOONS EXTRA VIRGIN
  OLIVE OIL, PLUS EXTRA FOR
  SERVING
1 CLOVE GARLIC, FINELY CHOPPED
2 TABLESPOONS FINELY CHOPPED
  FRESH FLAT-LEAF PARSLEY
90ML (3FLOZ) DRY WHITE WINE
300G (10½OZ) COOKED
  CHICKPEAS, WITH THEIR
  COOKING LIQUID
SALT AND FRESHLY GROUND
  BLACK PEPPER

Minestra alla Gonzaga

Spinach and asparagus soup

SERVES **6**

This is based on a recipe written in 1662 by Bartolomeo Stefani of Mantova.

Wash the spinach well and discard the stalks. Chop the spinach roughly. Cut off the asparagus tips and reserve; chop the stalks finely. Heat the stock to boiling.

In a saucepan melt the butter and fry the leeks for a few minutes. Add the fennel and the asparagus stalks and tips. Cook over a gentle heat for 10 minutes, stirring occasionally with a wooden spoon. Add the spinach to the pan and stir in, then add the hot stock. Season with salt. Leave the soup to cook, with the pan half covered, over a moderate heat for 1 hour, stirring occasionally.

Serve with croutons and Parmesan.

500G (1LB 2OZ) SPINACH
200G (7OZ) ASPARAGUS
1 LITRE (1¾ PINTS) VEGETABLE
  STOCK (SEE PAGE 56)
50G (1¾OZ) BUTTER
200G (7OZ) LEEKS, INCLUDING
  A LITTLE OF THE GREEN,
  FINELY CHOPPED
75G (2½OZ) FENNEL BULB,
  INCLUDING A FEW FRONDS,
  FINELY CHOPPED
SALT
CROUTONS
FRESHLY GRATED PARMESAN

PASTA & RICE

Spaghetti all'Astice

Spaghetti with lobster sauce

SERVES **4**

*This pasta recipe is an Italian way of making an expensive
ingredient, lobster, economical.*

Plunge the lobster into boiling salted water, bring the
water back to the boil and cook for 5 minutes. Remove
the lobster from the pot and plunge it into cold water to cool
it quickly. Twist off the claws, crack them and remove the
meat. Cut open the tail shell, cutting down the length of the
soft underside. Extract the meat from the shell and cut the
meat into cubes.

Fry the sun-dried tomatoes, garlic, parsley and chilli in the
olive oil. Add the wine and let it evaporate. Add the diced
tomato and cook for 20 minutes, stirring frequently. Season
with salt. Remove the sauce from the heat and keep hot.

Cook the spaghetti in abundant boiling lightly salted water
until *al dente*. Drain and tip into a large heated bowl. Add the
lobster to the sauce, then pour over the spaghetti and mix in
well. Add more chopped parsley, if liked, then serve.

1 LIVE LOBSTER, WEIGHING
ABOUT 800G (1¾LB)

2 SUN-DRIED TOMATOES PACKED
IN OIL, FINELY CHOPPED

1 CLOVE GARLIC, FINELY CHOPPED

2 TABLESPOONS FINELY CHOPPED
FRESH FLAT-LEAF PARSLEY

1 FRESH CHILLI, FINELY SLICED

125ML (4FLOZ) EXTRA VIRGIN
OLIVE OIL

½ WINEGLASS DRY WHITE WINE

4 RIPE TOMATOES, SKINNED,
SEEDED AND DICED

SALT

350G (12OZ) SPAGHETTI

Pappardelle con Frutti di Mare al Pesto

Pappardelle with seafood and pesto

Remove the greyish beard from around the scallops and also the blackish sac. Rinse the scallops under running cold water and dry on kitchen paper. Cut each scallop in half. Scrub the mussels, clams and cockles, removing any beards from the mussels, and rinse with cold water. Discard any that have cracked shells or open shells that do not close when tapped. If necessary, purge the clams (see page 67).

Combine the basil, pine nuts, 1 clove of garlic and a pinch of salt in a blender and work until smooth. Blend in enough olive oil to obtain a homogenous sauce.

Put the mussels, clams and cockles in a large saucepan, cover and set over a strong heat. When the shells are open, remove the pan from the heat. Discard any with unopened shells. Remove the flesh from the shells and keep covered; discard all the shells.

Fry the remaining garlic in 2 tablespoons of olive oil until golden, then discard the garlic. Add the scallops to the garlic-flavoured oil and fry gently, turning once, until light gold on both sides. Add the mussels, clams and cockles. Pour in the white wine and season with salt and pepper. Keep hot.

Cook the pasta in abundant boiling lightly salted water until *al dente*. Drain and tip into a large warmed bowl. Dress the pasta with the pesto. Add the seafood, mix in quickly and serve at once.

500G (1LB 2OZ) MIXED
  SEAFOOD (SCALLOPS, MUSSELS,
  CLAMS, COCKLES)
30 FRESH BASIL LEAVES
25G (1¾OZ) PINE NUTS
2 CLOVES GARLIC, PEELED
SALT AND FRESHLY GROUND
  BLACK PEPPER
EXTRA VIRGIN OLIVE OIL
1 LIQUEUR GLASS DRY WHITE
  WINE
400G (14OZ) FRESH PAPPARDELLE
FRESH DILL, TO GARNISH

Pennette alle 'Ciliegie'

PENNETTE WITH CHERRY TOMATOES

SERVES **4**

True mozzarella di bufala *is made from the milk of water buffaloes. If not available, you can use cow's milk mozzarella instead.*

Rinse the rocket and remove the stalks. Tear up the larger leaves. Rub a large serving bowl with the garlic, then discard the garlic. Place the rocket in the bowl and dress with the olive oil. Add the finely chopped chilli and cherry tomatoes and season with salt. Toss well to blend evenly.

Cook the pennette in boiling lightly salted water until *al dente*. Drain thoroughly and add to the bowl together with the mozzarella. Quickly mix together and serve at once.

1 BUNCH OF ROCKET, ABOUT 100G
(3½ OZ)

1 CLOVE GARLIC, PEELED

4 TABLESPOONS EXTRA VIRGIN
OLIVE OIL

1 FRESH CHILLI, FINELY CHOPPED

16 CHERRY TOMATOES,
PREFERABLY ON THE VINE
(THEY TEND TO BE RIPER),
SKINNED AND CUT IN HALF

SALT

320G (11½ OZ) PENNETTE

200G (7OZ) MOZZARELLA DI
BUFALA, DICED

RIGHT *Pennette alle 'Ciliegie'*

Spaghetti in Padella

Spaghetti with sausage and porcini sauce

SERVES 4

A very spicy appetizing dish to serve in winter.

Skin the sausages and put into a food processor with the Parma ham. Process until finely ground. In a saucepan fry the onion and garlic in the olive oil until soft and light gold. Add the sausage and Parma ham mixture and stir into the onion for a few minutes. Add the tomato passata. Leave to cook over a moderate heat for 1 hour, stirring occasionally.

Remove the mushrooms from their soaking water and chop them finely. Strain the soaking liquid through a fine sieve. Add the mushrooms and soaking liquid to the saucepan together with the chilli and a seasoning of pepper; taste to see if salt is needed. Cook the sauce for a further 15 minutes.

When the sauce is ready, transfer it to a large frying pan capable of holding the cooked spaghetti as well.

Cook the spaghetti in abundant boiling lightly salted water until just under *al dente*. Drain and add to the sausage sauce. Mix in thoroughly, then cook until the spaghetti is *al dente*. Mix the garlic and parsley together and sprinkle on top of the pasta with the Parmesan cheese. Serve at once.

400G (14OZ) SPAGHETTI

I CLOVE GARLIC, FINELY CHOPPED

4 TABLESPOONS FINELY CHOPPED
FRESH FLAT-LEAF PARSLEY

60G (2OZ) PARMESAN, FRESHLY
GRATED

For the sauce

3 SPICY ITALIAN SAUSAGES, ABOUT
250G (9OZ) IN TOTAL

100G (3½OZ) PARMA HAM, FINELY
DICED

I ONION, FINELY CHOPPED

I CLOVE GARLIC, FINELY CHOPPED

3 TABLESPOONS EXTRA VIRGIN
OLIVE OIL

600G (ILB 5OZ) TOMATO PASSATA

50G (1¾OZ) DRIED PORCINI
MUSHROOMS, SOAKED IN 300ML
(½ PINT) TEPID WATER FOR 30
MINUTES

I SMALL FRESH RED CHILLI,
FINELY SLICED

SALT AND FRESHLY GROUND
BLACK PEPPER

Conchiglie all'Anconetana
Conchiglie with sardines

SERVES **4**

Conchiglie are smallish shell-shaped pasta.

Remove the head, fins and tail from the sardines. Fry the garlic in the olive oil until golden, then add the sardines and break them up with a wooden spoon. Add the wine and allow to evaporate. Stir in the basil, parsley, salt and pepper. Cook for a few seconds, then remove from the heat and keep hot.

Cook the pasta in abundant boiling lightly salted water until *al dente*. Drain, tip into a large heated bowl and add the sardine sauce. Serve at once.

300G (10½ OZ) FRESH SARDINES, CLEANED, SCALED AND BONED

I CLOVE GARLIC, FINELY CHOPPED

6 TABLESPOONS EXTRA VIRGIN OLIVE OIL

½ WINEGLASS DRY WHITE WINE

16–20 FRESH BASIL LEAVES, TORN

4 TABLESPOONS FINELY CHOPPED FRESH FLAT-LEAF PARSLEY

SALT AND FRESHLY GROUND BLACK PEPPER

280G (10OZ) CONCHIGLIE

Pappardelle alla Ricotta
Pappardelle with ricotta

SERVES **4**

A quick recipe which can be served as a meal on its own.
Ideal for vegetarians.

In a bowl combine the julienne of sundried tomatoes, the whole black olives, oregano and olive oil. Stir well together, then set the mixture aside to macerate while you cook the pasta.

Cook the pappardelle in abundant boiling lightly salted water until *al dente*. Towards the end of the cooking time, ladle 125ml (4floz) of the pasta cooking water into a large bowl. Add the ricotta and mix well. Season generously with pepper. Drain the pappardelle, add to the ricotta mixture and mix gently together. Sprinkle the tomato and olive mixture and the basil on top and serve at once.

50G (1¾ OZ) SUN-DRIED TOMATOES, PACKED IN OLIVE OIL, CUT IN JULIENNE

50G (1¾ OZ) BLACK OLIVES, STONED

I TABLESPOON DRIED OREGANO

3 TABLESPOONS EXTRA VIRGIN OLIVE OIL

320G (11½ OZ) FRESH PAPPARDELLE

200G (7OZ) FRESH RICOTTA

SALT AND FRESHLY GROUND BLACK PEPPER

I BUNCH OF FRESH BASIL

Spaghetti alle Alghe con Salmone

Spaghetti with salmon and samphire

SERVES 4-6

Samphire grows on the salt marshes in Wales. It is wonderfully salty and succulent and has a taste of the sea. It is also good eaten raw, dressed with oil and lemon juice.

Sewin, or sea trout, which can be used instead of salmon, is an estuarine fish. My fishmonger tells me that thousands of years ago it originated from a brown trout crossed with a salmon.

200G (7OZ) FRESH SAMPHIRE
240–360G (9–12OZ) SPAGHETTI
(60G/2OZ PER PERSON)
2 SHALLOTS, FINELY CHOPPED
1 CLOVE GARLIC, FINELY CHOPPED
4 TABLESPOONS OLIVE OIL
30G (1OZ) BUTTER
100ML (3½ FLOZ) DRY WHITE
WINE
JUICE OF ½ LEMON
SALT AND FRESHLY GROUND
BLACK PEPPER
2 SLICES SALMON, WEIGHING
400G (14OZ) IN TOTAL, CUT
INTO 1CM/½IN DICE
200G (7OZ) PLUM TOMATOES,
SKINNED, SEEDED AND DICED

Clean the samphire carefully and thoroughly. Drop it into a saucepan of boiling water and blanch it for 1 minute. Drain the samphire in a colander and set aside.

Cook the spaghetti in plenty of boiling salted water until *al dente*. In the meantime, fry the shallots and garlic in the olive oil and butter until light gold. Add the white wine and boil to reduce by half. Season with the lemon juice, salt, if needed, and pepper.

Drain the spaghetti and tip it into a large heated bowl. Add the salmon to the sauce and stir to mix, then immediately pour the sauce over the spaghetti and toss well together. Add the fresh tomato cubes and samphire and mix in, then serve at once.

RIGHT *Spaghetti alle Alghe con Salmone*

Linguine alle Erbe e Scorzette di Limone

Linguine with herbs and lemon

SERVES **4**

Cut the lemon zest in julienne. Blanch the lemon zest in boiling water for 2 minutes, then refresh under cold water. Repeat this blanching operation twice more, then drain the zest on kitchen paper.

Chop the mint, fennel and parsley finely and put them to infuse in the extra virgin olive oil while you cook the pasta.

Cook the pasta in abundant boiling salted water until *al dente*. In the meantime, briefly brown the lemon julienne in the butter, and season with salt and pepper. Drain the pasta and tip into a large heated bowl. Add the lemon julienne and the herb oil and toss well. Serve at once.

THINLY PARED ZEST OF 2 LEMONS

1 LARGE SPRIG FRESH MINT

1 LARGE SPRIG FRESH HERB
  FENNEL

1 SMALL BUNCH OF PARSLEY

5 TABLESPOONS EXTRA VIRGIN
  OLIVE OIL

320G (11½OZ) FRESH LINGUINE

30G (1OZ) BUTTER

SALT AND FRESHLY GROUND
  BLACK PEPPER

LINGUINE CON LE LENTICCHIE
LINGUINE WITH LENTIL SAUCE

SERVES **4**

In Italy, on the feast day of San Silvestro, New Year's Eve, it is an absolute must that lentils are eaten. They are supposed to represent wealth. Is it because they look like money, or for their nutritive value, which has been held in great esteem since the time of ancient civilizations?

Fry the onion, carrot, celery and garlic in 4 tablespoons of the olive oil until soft. Add the lentils and stir in for a minute or two, then add the wine and allow to bubble away. Stir in the passata. Gently cook until the lentils are tender. This takes about 30 minutes, but very much depends on the age of the lentils. Season the sauce with salt and keep warm.

Cook the pasta in abundant boiling lightly salted water until *al dente*. In the meantime, heat the remaining 2 tablespoons of olive oil in a small pan and add the chillies. Drain the pasta and tip into a large heated bowl. Add the chilli oil and toss to coat. Pour the lentil sauce over the pasta, stir well and serve at once, with freshly grated Parmesan.

1 SMALL ONION, FINELY CHOPPED

1 SMALL CARROT, FINELY CHOPPED

½ STICK CELERY, FINELY CHOPPED

1 CLOVE GARLIC, FINELY CHOPPED

6 TABLESPOONS EXTRA VIRGIN OLIVE OIL

100G (3½OZ) DRIED LENTILS

½ WINEGLASS DRY WHITE WINE

200G (7OZ) TOMATO PASSATA

SALT

400G (14OZ) FRESH LINGUINE OR TRENETTE

½ SMALL FRESH RED CHILLI, FINELY CHOPPED

FRESHLY GRATED PARMESAN

Tagliolini con Carciofi e Prosciutto

TAGLIOLINI WITH ARTICHOKES AND PARMA HAM

SERVES 4

For this pasta dish, use the viola or violetti variety of globe artichokes. These are small and young, and have no hairy chokes (or very little), so once the outer leaves are removed the whole artichoke can be eaten. Although we have suggested using Parma ham rather than prosciutto *here and in other recipes, in the Marche* prosciutto di Carpegna *or* prosciutto nostrano *would be used.*

Preheat the oven to 200°C/400°F/gas 6. Wash and trim the artichokes, and remove the hard outer leaves. Cut each artichoke lengthways into 6 and drop into water that has been acidulated with the lemon juice.

Fry the spring onions and Parma ham in the olive oil in a small flameproof casserole. Add the drained artichokes and cook over a moderate heat for 10 minutes, stirring frequently. Add the wine and let it evaporate. Add ½ wineglass of water. Cover the casserole and transfer to the oven. Continue cooking for about 20 minutes or until the sauce is reduced and the artichokes are tender. Season with salt and pepper. (The sauce can be prepared in advance and then reheated for serving.)

Cook the pasta in abundant boiling lightly salted water until *al dente*. Drain and tip into a large warmed bowl. Pour the sauce over the pasta, add the parsley leaves and Parmesan shavings, and serve at once.

4 GLOBE ARTICHOKES

JUICE OF 1 LEMON

2 LARGE SPRING ONIONS, CHOPPED

50G (1¾OZ) PARMA HAM, CUT IN JULIENNE

4 TABLESPOONS EXTRA VIRGIN OLIVE OIL

½ WINEGLASS DRY WHITE WINE

SALT AND FRESHLY GROUND BLACK PEPPER

400G (14OZ) FRESH TAGLIOLINI

FRESH FLAT-LEAF PARSLEY

FRESHLY SHAVED PARMESAN

RIGHT *Tagliolini con Carciofi e Prosciutto*

Tagliatelle con Ragù di Coniglio

Tagliatelle with rabbit sauce

SERVES 6

Tagliatelle, a ribbon-shaped pasta, was invented by Mastro Zafirano who was cook to Conte Benvoglio when Lucrezia Borgia married Duke d'Este in 1487. The tagliatelle are supposed to represent Lucrezia's long blonde tresses. The exact width for tagliatelle – 1.5cm – is registered in the chamber of commerce in Bologna.

600G (1LB 5OZ) FRESH
  TAGLIATELLE OR PAPPARDELLE
FRESHLY GRATED PARMESAN
For the ragù
100G (3½OZ) PANCETTA, DICED
6 TABLESPOONS EXTRA VIRGIN
  OLIVE OIL
60G (2OZ) ONION, FINELY
  CHOPPED
60G (2OZ) CARROT, FINELY
  CHOPPED
60G (2OZ) CELERY, FINELY DICED
2 GARLIC CLOVES, FINELY
  CHOPPED
800G (1¾LB) JOINTED RABBIT,
  PREFERABLY THE HIND LEGS
2 SPRIGS FRESH ROSEMARY
1 BOUQUET GARNI
1 BUNCH OF PARSLEY
240ML (8FLOZ) CUP TOMATO
  PASSATA
½ WINEGLASS DRY WHITE WINE
SALT AND FRESHLY GROUND
  BLACK PEPPER

For the *ragù*, fry the pancetta in 4 tablespoons of olive oil in a frying pan, then add the onion, carrot, celery and garlic and cook until they are soft and golden. Transfer the pancetta and vegetables to a heavy flameproof casserole using a perforated spoon. Heat the remaining oil in the frying pan and fry the rabbit pieces until golden on all sides. Add the rabbit pieces to the casserole.

Tie the rosemary in a muslin bag and add to the casserole with the bouquet garni, parsley, tomato passata and wine. Bring gently to the boil. Add just enough hot water to cover the rabbit joints, and season with salt and pepper. Reduce the heat, cover and cook gently for 1 hour or until the rabbit is tender. (If the rabbit is farmed, the cooking time may be less.)

Remove the rabbit joints from the sauce. Take the meat off the bone and chop into dice. Return the diced meat to the sauce. Remove the herbs and check the seasoning. Make sure the sauce is of a dense consistency (boil it to reduce, if necessary).

Cook the pasta in abundant boiling salted water until *al dente*. Drain and serve with the rabbit sauce and a sprinkling of Parmesan.

Trenette alla Barba
di Frate e Prosciutto
TRENETTE WITH *BARBA DI FRATE* AND PARMA HAM

SERVES **4**

Barba di frate, *the young shoots of the salsify plant, can be replaced by fresh spinach if necessary.*

Fry the onion in the olive oil in a large saucepan until soft. Add the Parma ham and cook for a few more minutes. Remove from the heat and keep warm.

Cook the pasta with the *barba di frate* in abundant boiling lightly salted water until the pasta is *al dente*. Drain and add the pasta and greens to the Parma ham mixture. Toss over a high heat for a few minutes, then season with pepper and serve at once.

1 SMALL ONION, FINELY CHOPPED

4 TABLESPOONS EXTRA VIRGIN
  OLIVE OIL

50G (1¾OZ) PARMA HAM, CUT
  IN JULIENNE

SALT AND FRESHLY GROUND
  BLACK PEPPER

300G (10½OZ) FRESH
  TRENETTE

200G (7OZ) *BARBA DI FRATE*

Frittata di Maccheroni
FLAT PASTA OMELETTE

SERVES **4**

This is not a recipe in the normal sense. If you have some left-over spaghetti with bolognese sauce or Spaghetti in Padella *(page 42), this is a way of using it up. Double or triple the other ingredients, according to how much pasta you have.*

Mix the pasta, egg and cheese together. Heat a non-stick frying pan and tip in the pasta mixture. Press down with the back of a spoon to make a flat cake. Cook on both sides until golden, as one would for a flat omelette. Serve at once.

200G (7OZ) PASTA WITH SAUCE

1 EGG

1 TABLESPOON FRESHLY GRATED
  PARMESAN OR PECORINO

Ravioli di Baccalà

RAVIOLI STUFFED WITH SALT COD

SERVES **6-8**

*Italian flour type 'O' is obtainable in Italian delicatessens.
We use it when we make pasta with a hand machine or entirely by
hand. If you are unable to find flour type 'O', use strong white
flour instead. (Farina 'OO' is better for electric pasta machines.)*

To make the pasta dough, put the flour in a mound on a
work surface and make a hollow in the centre. Add a
little salt to the eggs and beat lightly with a fork, then pour
into the hollow. Draw the flour into the eggs until well amalgamated into a dough. If the dough seems too moist, add a
little more flour. Knead the dough with the heel of the palm
of the hand, keeping your fingers bent, folding the pasta in
half and giving it a half turn, then pushing it out again.
Continue kneading for 10 minutes. (Alternatively, the pasta
dough can be rolled through the rollers of a pasta machine set
at maximum width 4 or 5 times or until the dough is
smooth.) Cut the dough into 4 portions. Roll out each
portion thinly, either by hand or with a pasta machine. Keep
the dough covered with a damp cloth until required.

Cut the salt cod in cubes and cook in boiling water until
soft. Drain thoroughly. Work the cod with the garlic in a food
processor until smooth. Slowly add the olive oil through the
feed tube, to make a homogenous purée. Brush a sheet of
pasta with egg wash. Place teaspoons of the salt cod purée on
the sheet, spaced evenly apart. Place another sheet of pasta on
top and press down around the filling. Cut into ravioli with a
fluted round pastry cutter or using a pastry wheel. Make
ravioli from the remaining pasta and filling.

To make the sauce, heat the olive oil in a frying pan and
add the garlic and tomatoes. Stir round, then add the
marjoram, salt and pepper. Cook gently, stirring frequently,
for 10 minutes.

Cook the ravioli in abundant boiling lightly salted water
until just under *al dente*. Drain them using a perforated spoon
and add to the sauce. Cook for 2 more minutes and serve.

For the pasta
400G (14OZ) TYPE 'O' FLOUR
SALT
4 EGGS
BEATEN EGG MIXED WITH A
   FEW DROPS OF WATER, FOR
   EGG WASH
For the filling
500G (1LB 2OZ) DRIED SALT COD,
   SOAKED TO REHYDRATE AND
   THEN BONED
4 CLOVES GARLIC
175ML (6FLOZ) EXTRA VIRGIN
   OLIVE OIL
For the sauce
4 TABLESPOONS EXTRA VIRGIN
   OLIVE OIL
1 CLOVE GARLIC, FINELY CHOPPED
6 PLUM TOMATOES, SKINNED,
   SEEDED AND DICED
LEAVES FROM 1 SPRIG FRESH
   MARJORAM
SALT AND FRESHLY GROUND
   BLACK PEPPER

GNOCCHI DI PATATE

POTATO GNOCCHI

SERVES **4**

Do not be put off by the instructions for making gnocchi — it is not as complicated as it sounds. If you have a microwave oven, use it to cook the potatoes. Serve the gnocchi with duck sauce (see page 54) or lobster and mussel sauce (see page 55).

ABOUT 1.2KG (2¾LB) FLOURY
POTATOES
1 EGG
250G (9OZ) PLAIN FLOUR
A GENEROUS PINCH OF FRESHLY
GRATED NUTMEG
SALT AND FRESHLY GROUND
BLACK PEPPER

Cook the potatoes, in their skins, in boiling salted water. Drain and, as soon as they are cool enough to handle, peel them. Pass the warm potatoes immediately through a potato ricer or mouli-légumes. You should have 1kg (2¼lb) potato purée. Add the egg, flour, nutmeg and a seasoning of salt and pepper to the potato purée and work in well.

Take pieces of the potato mixture and roll into thumb-thick rolls, then cut into short cylinders 2–3cm (1–1¼in) long. Now, with the tip of the index finger, roll each cylinder over the inside curve of a long-pronged fork. While pressing the potato cylinder against the prongs with your finger, flip it away towards the handle of the fork, and then let it drop on to a lightly floured tray. This 'rolling' is what keeps the gnocchi light.

Cook the gnocchi in abundant boiling salted water. As soon as they rise to the surface, remove them with a perforated spoon.

Gnocchi di Patate con Sugo di Anitra

Potato gnocchi with duck sauce

SERVES 4

In the Marche region gnocchi are always served on a Thursday. Although I have tried to find out the reason for this, and have heard so many stories, I still do not know why.
This recipe is the most common in the area. In one form or another, duck used always to be served during the period of sowing and harvesting. It was traditionally given to the hired hands.

Fry the duck legs in 2 tablespoons of olive oil until golden all over. Transfer to a flameproof casserole. In a clean frying pan, fry the pancetta, onion, garlic, carrot and celery in the remaining olive oil. When softened add to the duck legs with the herbs. Season with salt and pepper. Add the wine and cook over a brisk flame until reduced. Add the tomato dice and the paste, stir and cook for a few minutes. Pour in enough water barely to cover the ingredients. Cover and leave to simmer gently for 45–60 minutes or until the duck is tender.

Remove the duck. Take the meat from the bones and chop the meat into small dice. Skim the sauce of any fat. Return the duck meat to the sauce, check the seasoning and remove the herbs. Serve with the hot potato gnocchi, sprinkled with Parmesan.

GNOCCHI DI PATATE (SEE PAGE 53), FRESHLY COOKED

FRESHLY GRATED PARMESAN

For the sauce

3 DUCK LEGS

4 TABLESPOONS EXTRA VIRGIN OLIVE OIL

4 SLICES PANCETTA, FINELY CHOPPED

½ ONION, FINELY CHOPPED

1 CLOVE GARLIC, FINELY CHOPPED

1 CARROT, FINELY CHOPPED

1 STICK CELERY, FINELY CHOPPED

2 SPRIGS PARSLEY

2 SPRIGS FRESH MARJORAM

1 BAY LEAF

SALT AND FRESHLY GROUND BLACK PEPPER

½ WINEGLASS DRY WHITE WINE

500G (1LB 2OZ) TOMATOES, SKINNED, SEEDED AND DICED

2 TABLESPOONS TOMATO PASTE

Gnocchi di Patate con Sugo di Astice

Potato gnocchi with lobster and mussel sauce

Gnocchi are a form of dumpling but much lighter, potatoes being the most predominant ingredient.

Scrub the mussels and remove any beards. Discard any mussels with broken shells or open shells that do not close when tapped. Put the mussels in a large pan with 400ml (14floz) of the wine and the finely chopped garlic. Cover the pan and set over high heat. Cook, shaking the pan every now and then, until the mussels open. Discard any mussels that remain stubbornly closed. Remove the mussels from the shells, reserving 8 in their shell for decoration. Set the mussels aside.

Filter the mussel cooking liquid into a clean pan and add the tomatoes, whole garlic cloves, olive oil and abundant pepper. Cook for 10 minutes, stirring occasionally. In the meantime, remove the lobster meat from the shell and chop into bite-sized pieces. Add the lobster to the tomato sauce together with the shelled mussels, remaining wine, spring onions and herbs. Taste and season with salt (the mussel liquor may be salty enough). Heat the lobster through on a brisk heat. Remove the garlic.

Serve with the hot gnocchi, garnished with the mussels in their shells.

GNOCCHI DI PATATE (SEE PAGE 53), FRESHLY COOKED

For the sauce

2KG (4½LB) MUSSELS

600ML (1 PINT) DRY WHITE WINE

4 CLOVES GARLIC, 2 PEELED AND 2 FINELY CHOPPED

700G (1LB 9OZ) TOMATOES, SKINNED, SEEDED AND DICED

150ML (¼ PINT) EXTRA VIRGIN OLIVE OIL

SALT AND FRESHLY GROUND BLACK PEPPER

2 BOILED LOBSTER, EACH WEIGHING ABOUT 800G (1¾LB)

4 SPRING ONIONS, FINELY CHOPPED

2 TABLESPOONS FINELY CHOPPED PARSLEY

2 TABLESPOONS FINELY TORN FRESH BASIL

Risotto ai Porri

Risotto with leeks

SERVES 6

Although this is an Italian recipe, it has a Welsh taste.

Heat the vegetable stock in a saucepan to boiling. Heat the olive oil in a shallow flameproof casserole and fry the onion gently until translucent, making sure it does not colour. Add the pancetta and leeks and mix into the onion. Add the rice and stir it in thoroughly but gently, so as to absorb the oil. Fry for 5 minutes, stirring. Add the wine and cook until it has been absorbed.

Start adding the stock, a ladle at a time, and cook, stirring constantly with a wooden spoon. As each addition of stock is absorbed, add more. This process will take about 20 minutes. When all the stock has been added and absorbed, the rice should be *al dente*. Remove the risotto from the heat and add the butter, in bits, and the Parmesan. Mix well, then leave to rest for a few minutes before serving.

1.2 LITRES (2 PINTS) VEGETABLE STOCK (SEE BELOW)

4 TABLESPOONS EXTRA VIRGIN OLIVE OIL

1 ONION, FINELY CHOPPED

150G (5½OZ) SMOKED PANCETTA, CUT IN JULIENNE

200G (7OZ) LEEKS, THINLY SLICED, INCLUDING SOME OF THE GREEN

420G (15OZ) RISOTTO RICE (ARBORIO)

200ML (7FLOZ) DRY WHITE WINE

60G (2OZ) BUTTER, SOFTENED

80G (3OZ) PARMESAN, FRESHLY GRATED

Vegetable Stock

MAKES ABOUT 1.2 LITRES (2 PTS)

This recipe is a good base for any vegetarian soup, risotto, etc., requiring stock.

Roughly chop the vegetables. Heat a little oil in a large saucepan, add the vegetables and cover. Sweat over a low heat until the vegetables are very soft but not coloured. Pour in 1.5 litres (2¾ pints) hot water and add the bouquet garni, a little salt and the peppercorns. Bring to the boil, then reduce the heat and simmer for 2 hours. Strain the stock.

450G (1LB) ONIONS

450G (1LB) CARROTS

450 (1LB) LEEKS

4 STICKS CELERY

OLIVE OIL

1 BOUQUET GARNI

SALT

A FEW BLACK PEPPERCORNS

Risotto alla Rossini

RISOTTO WITH PORCINI AND BEEF MARROW

SERVES **4**

The composer Rossini was a gourmet as well as a composer, and he created and recorded many recipes. The following is very common in the Marche.

Heat the stock in a saucepan to boiling. Melt 50g (1¾oz) of the butter in a wide flameproof casserole, add the beef marrow and cook until the fat is rendered. Add the rice and stir into the butter and marrow for a few minutes until the butter and marrow have been absorbed. Season with salt. Start adding the hot stock, a ladle at a time, and cook stirring constantly. As each addition of stock is absorbed, add more. This process will take about 20 minutes. Half way through cooking add the tomato dice. When all the stock has been added and absorbed, the rice should be *al dente*.

Towards the end of cooking, fry the porcini in the remaining butter, which must be hot and foaming. Season with salt and pepper.

Stir the grated Parmesan into the egg yolks and add to the cooked risotto. Stir in thoroughly over a gentle heat. Serve the risotto with the porcini on top and finish with shavings of Parmesan.

850ML (1½ PINTS) RICH MEAT STOCK

100G (3½ OZ) BUTTER

70G (2½ OZ) BEEF MARROW, SIEVED

400G (14OZ) RISOTTO RICE (CARNAROLI)

SALT AND FRESHLY GROUND BLACK PEPPER

4 TOMATOES, SKINNED, SEEDED AND DICED

250G (9OZ) FRESH PORCINI MUSHROOMS, CHOPPED

4 TABLESPOONS FRESHLY GRATED PARMESAN

2 EGG YOLKS, LIGHTLY BEATEN

FRESHLY SHAVED PARMESAN

Panzerotti Fritti

Deep-fried mozzarella pastries

SERVES 4–6

Panzerotti *are a speciality of Puglia, which, like the Marche, is on the Adriatic coast.*

To make the pastry dough, put the flour into a bowl and make a hollow in the centre. Add the butter, egg yolk, milk and salt to the hollow. Work the ingredients together with your fingertips to make a dough. Cover the bowl with a cloth and leave the dough to rest at room temperature for 30 minutes.

Roll out the pastry dough on a floured board into an oblong shape. Fold the dough twice back on itself, then cover again and leave once more for 30 minutes.

Mix together the ingredients for the filling.

Roll out the pastry dough until 3mm (⅛in) thick. Cut it into two equal pieces. Brush one sheet with the egg wash. Dot blobs of the filling in rows on the egg-washed sheet, leaving a space of 3cm (1¼in) between the blobs. Brush the second sheet of pastry with egg wash and lay it over the first sheet, egg-washed side down. Using a finger, press down around the blobs of filling, then cut into squares or oblongs using a pastry wheel. Press with a finger all around the edges to ensure the *panzerotti* are well sealed. Put the *panzerotti* on a floured cloth as they are prepared.

Brush the *panzerotti* with egg wash, then deep fry in hot olive oil for about 6 minutes, turning to cook and colour evenly. Drain on kitchen paper and serve at once, sprinkled with salt.

For the pastry

200G (7OZ) PLAIN FLOUR

100G (3½ OZ) BUTTER, DICED

1 EGG YOLK

2 TABLESPOONS MILK

SALT

For the filling

200G (7OZ) MOZZARELLA, FINELY
  DICED

50G (1¼ OZ) PARMA HAM, CUT IN
  JULIENNE

30G (1OZ) PARMESAN, FRESHLY
  GRATED

2 EGGS

A GOOD PINCH OF FINELY
  CHOPPED PARSLEY

A SMALL PINCH OF FRESHLY
  GRATED NUTMEG

SALT AND FRESHLY GROUND
  BLACK PEPPER

To finish

1 EGG BEATEN WITH A FEW DROPS
  OF WATER, FOR THE EGG WASH

LIGHT OLIVE OIL FOR DEEP FRYING

SALT

GLI STRACCI DI ANTRODOCO

BEEF-STUFFED PANCAKES WITH TOMATO SAUCE

SERVES **8–10**

First make the pancakes. Crack the eggs into a bowl and add 6 half egg-shells of cold water, the sifted flour and salt. Beat together until a light batter is obtained.

Melt a little butter in a non-stick frying pan measuring 18cm (7in) in diameter; pour out excess butter to leave a film. Pour in a ladle of the batter and swirl it round to make a thin pancake. Cook on both sides, then tip out of the pan. Continue making pancakes until all the batter is used up. It will make approximately 20 pancakes. Set aside.

For the sauce, heat the olive oil in a saucepan and add the puréed tomatoes and the tomato paste mixture. Season with salt and pepper. Simmer the tomato sauce, stirring constantly, until well reduced and thickened.

In the meantime, fry the minced beef in a little butter. Season with salt and pepper.

Preheat the oven to 230°C/450°F/gas 8. Cover each pancake with a veil of tomato sauce and scatter over a table-spoon of minced meat, a few dice of mozzarella and a sprinkling of pecorino. Roll up the pancakes loosely and arrange in a buttered gratin dish. Cover with the remaining tomato sauce and scatter a few flakes of butter and abundant pecorino over the top. Bake for 15 minutes or until the surface is golden brown.

300G (10½ OZ) MINCED LEAN
   BEEF (SIRLOIN OR FILLET)
100G (3½ OZ) BUTTER
150G (5½ OZ) MOZZARELLA,
   FINELY DICED
100G (3½ OZ) PECORINO OR
   PARMESAN, FRESHLY GRATED
For the pancakes
12 EGGS
12 TABLESPOONS PLAIN FLOUR
A PINCH OF SALT
BUTTER
For the sauce
2 TABLESPOONS OLIVE OIL
600G (1LB 5OZ) RIPE TOMATOES,
   SKINNED AND PURÉED IN A
   BLENDER
1 TEASPOON TOMATO PASTE
   MIXED WITH A LITTLE BOILING
   WATER
SALT AND FRESHLY GROUND
   BLACK PEPPER

POLENTA PASTICCIATA

LAYERED POLENTA, MUSHROOM AND FONTINA PIE

SERVES **6**

Instant polenta flour could be used here – although not quite as good as ordinary polenta, it is not a bad substitute. An electric polenta maker is now available, which will take the labour out of the dish.

300G (10½OZ) POLENTA FLOUR
(MAIZEMEAL)

100G (3½OZ) BUTTER

500G (1LB 2OZ) BUTTON
MUSHROOMS, SLICED

SALT AND FRESHLY GROUND
BLACK PEPPER

30G (1OZ) TOMATO PASTE
MIXED WITH A LITTLE WATER

200G (7OZ) FONTINA, CUT IN
SLIVERS

100G (3½OZ) PARMESAN,
FRESHLY GRATED

Bring 1.5 litres (2¾ pints) of salted water to the boil. Gradually add the polenta to the boiling water (the water must be boiling because a high temperature is needed to burst the starch grains), letting the polenta drop in like sand sifting through your fingers. As the polenta is falling into the water, stir with a wooden spoon. Always stir in one direction, so that lumps will not occur. Reduce the heat and cook for 30–40 minutes, preferably stirring constantly. You should end up with quite a thick mixture. Pour the polenta on to an oiled surface and spread out to a thickness of 2cm (¾in). Leave to get cold.

When the polenta has set, slice it horizontally into three with a long-bladed knife or a piece of strong cotton, which is more traditional. You will be left with thin sheets of polenta.

Melt the butter and, when foaming, add the mushrooms. Quickly fry, then season with salt and pepper. Add the tomato paste mixture and cook, stirring, until amalgamated.

Preheat the oven to 220°C/425°F/gas 7. Put a layer of polenta in a baking tray. Spread with a third of the mushrooms, a third of the fontina cheese slivers and a third of the Parmesan scattered over. Put the second layer of polenta on top and repeat the mushrooms and cheese. Cover with the last layer of polenta and finish with the remaining mushrooms and cheese. Bake for 30 minutes or until the top is golden. Serve hot, cut into large squares.

FISH DISHES

Sgombri alla Pugliese
Mackerel with mint, garlic and chilli

SERVES **4**

This dish is good served with new potatoes that have been boiled in their skins and left to cool.

Remove the head and fins from the mackerel, then fillet them, making sure no stray bones are left. Score the skin of each fillet twice. Steam the fillets until just cooked through – about 5 minutes. Put the fillets in a shallow dish close together. Cover with the vinegar and leave to marinate for 1 hour.

Drain the vinegar away. Season the mackerel fillets with salt and pepper and the chilli flakes. Scatter the garlic and mint over the fillets. Drizzle with the extra virgin olive oil. Serve with wedges of lemon.

4 MACKEREL, WEIGHING
   800G (1¾LB) IN TOTAL
200ML (7FLOZ) WHITE WINE
   VINEGAR
SALT AND FRESHLY GROUND
   BLACK PEPPER
A PINCH OF DRIED CHILLI FLAKES
2 CLOVES GARLIC, FINELY
   CHOPPED
25 FRESH MINT LEAVES, ROUGHLY
   CHOPPED
2 TABLESPOONS EXTRA VIRGIN
   OLIVE OIL
4 LEMON WEDGES

Sardine Crude Marinate
Marinated sardines

SERVES **4**

Remove the heads from the sardines, then scale, eviscerate and bone them (or have your fishmonger do this for you). Rinse the fish and dry them with a cloth. Rub a very large, flat porcelain dish with the garlic. Arrange the fish on the dish, opened flat, skin side up, in one layer. Pour the vinegar or lemon juice over the fish. Cover the dish and leave in the fridge for 24 hours.

Drain the fish and give a rinse with fresh vinegar or lemon juice. Serve the sardines sprinkled with the parsley, finely chopped garlic, freshly ground black pepper and the olive oil.

500G (1LB 2OZ) FRESH SARDINES
2 CLOVES GARLIC, 1 HALVED AND
   1 FINELY CHOPPED
350ML (12FLOZ) WHITE WINE
   VINEGAR OR LEMON JUICE
2 TABLESPOONS FINELY CHOPPED
   PARSLEY
FRESHLY GROUND BLACK PEPPER
2 TABLESPOONS EXTRA VIRGIN
   OLIVE OIL

ALICI MARINATE

MARINATED ANCHOVIES

SERVES 6

To prepare the anchovies, remove the head with a decisive pull, so that you pull out the intestine at the same time. Put a slight pressure along the ventral side and open the fish up like a book. Pull out the back bone from the head to the tail, holding the fish in a slight curve. The bones will come away easily without damaging the flesh. Rinse the anchovies under cold running water and dry them on a clean cloth.

Cover the bottom of a large flat porcelain dish with half the chopped garlic and thyme. Place the anchovies in the dish, opened flat, skin side up, side by side. Cover the anchovies with vinegar and leave to marinate for at least 3 hours.

Drain the anchovies and put them in a clean dish. Cover the fish with extra virgin olive oil and sprinkle over the remaining garlic and thyme.

500G (1LB 2OZ) FRESH ANCHOVIES

2 CLOVES GARLIC, FINELY CHOPPED

2 TABLESPOONS FINELY CHOPPED FRESH THYME

WHITE WINE VINEGAR

EXTRA VIRGIN OLIVE OIL

FRITTURA DI CODE DI SCAMPI E ZUCCHINI

DEEP-FRIED SCAMPI AND COURGETTES

SERVES 4

Lightly coat the scampi and courgette chips with flour. Heat abundant olive oil in a deep pan and add the garlic. When the garlic has become light brown, remove it and discard. Fry the scampi in the hot oil until golden brown, turning them with a long-handled fork so that they cook and colour evenly. Remove with a slotted spoon and drain on kitchen paper. Keep hot while you fry the courgette chips in the same way.

Serve hot, sprinkled with salt and with wedges of lemon.

350G (12OZ) RAW SCAMPI (LANGOUSTINE) TAILS, PEELED

100G (3½OZ) COURGETTES, CUT IN THIN CHIPS

PLAIN FLOUR

LIGHT OLIVE OIL FOR FRYING

1 CLOVE GARLIC, PEELED

SALT

4 LEMON WEDGES

Triglie all'Aceto
Red mullet in vinegar

SERVES **4**

Red mullet has lean, firm flesh, making it perfect for this preparation. As it is cooked just in the retained heat of the boiling vinegar as it cools, be sure to use very fresh fish.

Remove the scales from the red mullet, either with the back of a knife or using a fish descaler. Eviscerate the mullet and remove the head; fillet the fish.

Heat the vinegar with the water and ½ teaspoon salt in a non-metallic pan. Put the fish fillets in a dish in one layer and scatter over the parsley sprigs, coriander seeds or peppercorns and the spring onions. Pour the boiling vinegar mixture over the fish. Leave to marinate for 1 hour.

Remove the fish from the marinade and arrange on the plates. Add some of the spring onions, drained, a few drops of extra virgin olive oil and a sprinkling of salt. Garnish with a few leaves of flat-leaf parsley or a wedge of lemon.

4 RED MULLET, WEIGHING
155–200G (5½–7OZ) EACH
1 WINEGLASS RED WINE VINEGAR
½ WINEGLASS WATER
SALT
A FEW SPRIGS PARSLEY
1 TEASPOON CORIANDER SEEDS
  OR BLACK PEPPERCORNS
8 SPRING ONIONS, THINLY SLICED
EXTRA VIRGIN OLIVE OIL
FLAT-LEAF PARSLEY OR LEMON
  WEDGES, TO GARNISH

RIGHT *Triglie all'Aceto*

Arrosto di Frutti di Mare alla Gallese

BAKED SEAFOOD WITH LAVERBREAD

SERVES **4**

Open the scallops and remove the flesh. Remove the greyish beard around the scallops and also the blackish sac. Rinse the scallops under cold water and dry on kitchen paper. Scrub the concave shell halves, and return the scallops to them.

Scrub the clams and purge them, if necessary (see page 67). Open the clams with a knife and remove the empty top shells. Scrub the mussels well and remove any beards. Discard mussels that have cracked shells or open shells that do not close when tapped. Steam open the mussels and razor shells in a shallow pan over a brisk heat with a little white wine added. As soon as the shells open, remove and discard the empty half shell. Chop the razor meat roughly and return to the half shell.

Split the scampi in half lengthways and remove the dark intestinal vein. Put all the seafood onto a large baking tray.

Preheat the oven to 200°C/400°F/gas 6. Fry the pancetta in 2 tablespoons olive oil until the fat runs. Add the breadcrumbs and stir into the pancetta and oil mixture. Season the seafood lightly with salt and pepper. Coat each piece of seafood with laverbread using a teaspoon. Sprinkle the pancetta and breadcrumb mixture on top, then drizzle with the remaining olive oil.

Bake for 10 minutes or until golden on top. Serve hot with lemon wedges.

4 SCALLOPS, IN SHELL
8 CLAMS (PALOURDES)
24 MUSSELS
8 RAZOR SHELLS
DRY WHITE WINE
12 RAW SCAMPI (LANGOUSTINES)
100G (3½ OZ) SMOKED PANCETTA, FINELY CHOPPED
4 TABLESPOONS EXTRA VIRGIN OLIVE OIL
200G (7OZ) DAY-OLD BREADCRUMBS
SALT AND FRESHLY GROUND BLACK PEPPER
200G (7OZ) LAVERBREAD
1 LEMON, CUT IN 4 WEDGES

Guazzetto di Pesce dell'Adriatico in Bianco

Mixed fish in the adriatic style

SERVES 4

This is another fish stew-soup found on the Adriatic coast, predominantly in the Marche region.

Peel the prawns and scampi. Cut them in half lengthways and remove the dark intestinal vein.

Remove the scales from the seabass. Eviscerate and skin it, then cut into 4 cutlets. Clean and skin the monkfish, and cut into 4 fillets. Remove the grey membrane. Clean and bone the whiting, cutting into 4 fillets. Remove the scales from the mullet, eviscerate and fillet. Reserve all the bones and trimmings from the fish, including the monkfish head.

Scrub the clams and purge them, if necessary (leave in a bucket of cold water, with a handful of fine oatmeal stirred in, for an hour or two). Scrub the mussels well, and remove any beards. Discard mussels that have cracked shells or open shells that do not close when tapped.

To make the fish stock, put the oil and vegetables in a large saucepan and cook until softened. Add all the reserved fish bones and trimmings, with the head of the monkfish, and fry in the oil and vegetable mixture. Pour in the wine and 1.5 litres (2¾ pints) water and add a little salt. Simmer for 30 minutes, skimming regularly. Strain the stock into a clean pan and boil to reduce by half.

In a large shallow saucepan fry the onion and garlic in the olive oil for 2 minutes. Add the prawns and scampi and briefly fry, then add the wine and cook until evaporated. Add 2 or 3 ladles of the fish stock and all the remaining fish previously seasoned. Cook for 3 minutes. Add the clams and the mussels and cook until the shells have opened, shaking the pan regularly. Sprinkle with parsley and freshly ground black pepper.

Serve with bruschetta (slices of bread cooked on a griddle and rubbed with garlic and a drizzle of extra virgin olive oil).

8 RAW KING OR TIGER PRAWNS

8 SCAMPI (LANGOUSTINES)

1 X 1KG (2¼ LB) SEABASS

1 X 1KG (2¼ LB) MONKFISH, WITH THE HEAD ON

2 SMALL WHITING

4 SMALL RED MULLET

40 CLAMS

20 MUSSELS

1 TABLESPOON FINELY CHOPPED ONION

½ TABLESPOON FINELY CHOPPED GARLIC

100ML (3½ FLOZ) EXTRA VIRGIN OLIVE OIL

1 WINEGLASS DRY WHITE WINE

SALT AND FRESHLY GROUND BLACK PEPPER

30G (1OZ) PARSLEY, FINELY CHOPPED

BRUSCHETTA, TO SERVE

For the fish stock

4 TABLESPOONS EXTRA VIRGIN OLIVE OIL

50G (1¾ OZ) ONION, ROUGHLY CHOPPED

50G (1¾ OZ) CELERY, ROUGHLY CHOPPED

50G (1¾ OZ) CARROT, ROUGHLY CHOPPED

50G (1¾ OZ) LEEK, ROUGHLY CHOPPED

1 WINEGLASS DRY WHITE WINE

BRODETTO DI GAMBERI

PRAWNS IN SAFFRON AND GARLIC SAUCE

SERVES 4

These prawns can be served just with crostini of bread, but another equally good way to serve them is with Campofilone maccheroncini (see page 20). Pour the prawns and sauce over the noodles and quickly toss together.

Prepare the prawns by cutting them open down the curved back (be careful not to cut right through) and opening them like a book. Remove the dark intestinal vein. Fry the garlic in the olive oil until lightly coloured. Add the prawns and tomato paste and fry briskly until the prawns have turned pink. Season generously with salt and pepper. Add the wine and reduce to zero. Add the saffron and water mixture and stir, then cook for a few more minutes. Remove the prawns and keep warm. Reduce the sauce until it is thick and homogenous. Pour the sauce over the prawns, sprinkle with the parsley and serve at once.

ABOUT 900G (2LB) RAW TIGER
PRAWNS IN SHELL, OR USE
MEDITERRANEAN PRAWNS

4 CLOVES GARLIC, FINELY
CHOPPED

125ML (4FLOZ) EXTRA VIRGIN
OLIVE OIL

4 LEVEL TABLESPOONS TOMATO
PASTE

SALT AND FRESHLY GROUND
BLACK PEPPER

450ML (16FLOZ) DRY WHITE WINE

A PINCH OF SAFFRON THREADS,
SOAKED IN 450ML (16FLOZ) WARM
WATER

1 TABLESPOOON CHOPPED FRESH
FLAT-LEAF PARSLEY

RIGHT *Brodetto di Gamberi*

TRIGLIE CON SCHIACCIATA DI PATATE

RED MULLET FILLETS WITH POTATO CAKES AND SAGE

SERVES **4**

Putting sage with mullet is a very traditional Marchigiani method.

To make the potato cakes, cook the potatoes, in their skins, in boiling salted water. Drain the potatoes and peel while they are still warm. Pass them through a potato ricer or mouli-légumes to make a purée. Sweat the leeks and cabbage in a little olive oil and butter. Add a little water to finish the cooking. Add the leeks and cabbage to the potato, season with salt and pepper, and mix together thoroughly. Divide the potato mixture into 4 and shape each portion into a flat cake. Lightly flour the cakes and set aside.

Fry the mullet fillets, skin side down, in a little olive oil in a non-stick frying pan for 30–40 seconds. Season with salt and pepper, then turn the fillets over and cook for 1 minute or so until cooked through. At the same time as the fish is cooking, fry the potato cakes in a little olive oil in another non-stick pan.

To serve, put a potato cake on each plate and place 3 fillets lightly on top. Drizzle with a little olive oil, sprinkle with parsley and scatter deep-fried sage leaves on top.

12 RED MULLET FILLETS, SKIN SCALED

EXTRA VIRGIN OLIVE OIL

SALT AND FRESHLY GROUND BLACK PEPPER

1 TABLESPOON FINELY CHOPPED FRESH FLAT-LEAF PARSLEY

24 FRESH SAGE LEAVES, DEEP FRIED IN OLIVE OIL

For the potato cakes

4 MEDIUM POTATOES SUITABLE FOR MASHING

100G (3½OZ) LEEKS, FINELY SLICED

100G (3½OZ) CABBAGE LEAVES, BOILED AND ROUGHLY CHOPPED

EXTRA VIRGIN OLIVE OIL

BUTTER

SALT AND FRESHLY GROUND BLACK PEPPER

PLAIN FLOUR

Coda di Rospo in Potacchio

Monkfish with garlic and tomato-wine sauce

SERVES 4

'In potacchio' is a style of cooking peculiar to the Marche region. The word comes from the French, potage *(soup).*

Cook the garlic cloves in boiling water until *al dente*. Drain. Heat a veil of olive oil in a large frying pan and fry the monkfish pieces with the garlic until golden. Add the wine and reduce until evaporated. Add the passata and sprigs of rosemary. Season with salt and pepper. Gently simmer the fish over moderately low heat for 8–10 minutes or until cooked. Serve the fish with the sauce and garlic cloves.

24 CLOVES GARLIC, PEELED

EXTRA VIRGIN OLIVE OIL

4 PIECES BONELESS MONKFISH, WEIGHING 200G (7OZ) EACH

I WINEGLASS DRY WHITE WINE

750ML (1¼ PINTS) TOMATO PASSATA

4 SPRIGS FRESH ROSEMARY

SALT AND FRESHLY GROUND BLACK PEPPER

Tonno 'Briaco' alla Marchigiana

Pan-fried tuna tournedos

SERVES 4

A very old Marchigiani recipe. Briaco *comes from the word* ubriaco, *meaning drunk.*

Heat a little olive oil in a frying pan, add the anchovy fillets and stir with a wooden spoon until broken down. Add the lemon juice, capers and bay leaf.

Fry the tuna in a little hot olive oil until just barely cooked through. Season with salt and pepper, then remove from the pan and keep warm.

Deglaze the pan with the Marsala and a little water, stirring well, and reduce the sauce to a glaze. Add the caper sauce and reduce slightly. Place the tuna on the fried bread and pour the sauce over. Sprinkle the parsley on top and serve at once.

EXTRA VIRGIN OLIVE OIL

8 ANCHOVY FILLETS PRESERVED IN OIL

JUICE OF I LARGE LEMON, FILTERED

I TABLESPOON SMALL SALTED CAPERS, WELL RINSED

I BAY LEAF

4 TUNA STEAKS CUT FROM TAIL END, WEIGHING 175G (6OZ) EACH

SALT AND FRESHLY GROUND BLACK PEPPER

150ML (¼FLOZ) DRY MARSALA

4 SLICES BREAD, THE SAME SIZE AS THE TUNA STEAKS, FRIED IN OLIVE OIL

I TABLESPOON FINELY CHOPPED PARSLEY

Cestini di Frutti di Mare

Seafood in spaghetti baskets

400G (14OZ) SQUID

400G (14OZ) RAW KING PRAWNS

400G (14OZ) MUSSELS

EXTRA VIRGIN OLIVE OIL

I CLOVE GARLIC, FINELY CHOPPED

I TABLESPOON CHOPPED PARSLEY

SALT AND FRESHLY GROUND
  BLACK PEPPER

½ WINEGLASS DRY WHITE WINE

50G (1¾OZ) BUTTER, CUT IN
  SMALL PIECES

For the spaghetti baskets

250G (9OZ) SPAGHETTI

2 TABLESPOONS EXTRA VIRGIN
  OLIVE OIL

OLIVE OIL FOR DEEP FRYING

Break up the spaghetti, and cook in a large pan of boiling lightly salted water until *al dente*. Drain the pasta and dress with the extra virgin olive oil. Leave to go cold.

Wash and skin the squid. Remove the ink sacs, eyes and mouths, and cut the bodies into rings. Set aside, with the tentacles. Peel the prawns, remove the intestinal vein and set aside.

Scrub the mussels well, and remove any beards. Discard mussels that have cracked shells or open shells that do not close when tapped. Put the cleaned mussels in a large pan with a little olive oil. Cook, shaking the pan occasionally, until the shells open. Remove the mussels from the shells (discard any mussels that remain stubbornly closed). Filter the cooking liquid and reserve.

Divide the cold spaghetti into 12 heaps. Put a heap of spaghetti into a potato-nest basket and clip the top piece over. Deep fry the spaghetti basket in hot olive oil until golden. Lift out of the oil and remove gently from the mould. Drain on kitchen paper. Repeat the operation until all the spaghetti is used up, to make 12 baskets.

Cook the prawns in 2 tablespoons of olive oil with the garlic for 3–4 minutes. In another pan, fry the squid in a little olive oil. Add the prawns, mussels and parsley to the squid, and season with salt and pepper. Using a perforated spoon, divide the seafood among the spaghetti baskets. Keep warm. Add the reserved mussel liquid and white wine to the seafood cooking juices and boil to reduce to a sauce. Add the butter and cook gently for a further 2 minutes. Pour the sauce over the seafood and serve.

RIGHT *Cestini di Frutti di Mare*

Tournedos di Pescatrice allo Speck

Tournedos of monkfish wrapped in pancetta

SERVES **4**

Pancetta is Italian streaky bacon, either smoked or unsmoked, cured for about 3 weeks and then air-dried for up to 4 months.

Preheat the oven to 150°C/300°F/gas 2. Cut the monkfish across into 8 tournedos. Wrap 2 slices of pancetta round each tournedos and secure with a wooden cocktail stick.

Heat the oil in a large flameproof baking dish over a low heat. Add the spring onions and cook for 1 minute. Add the fish and lightly season with salt, then raise the heat. Fry the fish to sear on both sides. Add the white wine and rosemary to the fish. Put the dish in the oven and cook for 5 minutes.

Arrange the tournedos on a serving dish, remove the sticks and keep warm. Add the lemon juice to the cooking juices in the baking dish, strain and pour over the tournedos. Dot the tomato dice round the plate and serve.

1.2KG (2¾LB) BONELESS MONKFISH

16 SLICES PANCETTA, CUT THINLY

2 TABLESPOONS EXTRA VIRGIN OLIVE OIL

2 SPRING ONIONS, CUT INTO 1CM (½IN) LENGTHS

SALT

2 WINEGLASSES DRY WHITE WINE

NEEDLES FROM 1 SPRIG FRESH ROSEMARY

JUICE OF ½ LEMON

2 RIPE TOMATOES, SKINNED, SEEDED AND CUT IN SMALL DICE

Cape Sante Gratinate

Gratinéed scallops in shell

SERVES **4**

Open the scallops and remove them from the shell. Wash and reserve the concave shell halves. Remove the greyish beard around the scallops, and also the blackish sac. Rinse the scallops under cold running water and dry on kitchen paper.

Preheat the grill. Mix together the breadcrumbs, Parmesan, parsley and garlic. Add 1 tablespoon of the olive oil and season with salt and pepper. Mix well.

Put the scallops into the concave shell halves. Divide the crumb mixture evenly among the scallops and drizzle the remaining olive oil over them. Set the shells on a baking tray and grill for 10 minutes. Serve hot, with lemon wedges.

8 FRESH SCALLOPS IN THEIR SHELLS

30G (1OZ) FRESH BREADCRUMBS

20G (¾OZ) PARMESAN, FRESHLY GRATED

2 TABLESPOONS FINELY CHOPPED PARSLEY

1 SMALL CLOVE GARLIC, FINELY CHOPPED

3 TABLESPOONS EXTRA VIRGIN OLIVE OIL

SALT AND FRESHLY GROUND BLACK PEPPER

4 LEMON WEDGES

Rombo al Marsala

Turbot fillets in marsala sauce

SERVES 4

Marsala, the Italian fortified wine, is available sweet – for use in desserts such as zabaglione – and dry (Marsala Secco). It takes its name from the town of Marsala in Sicily, where John Woodhouse, a Liverpudlian merchant, took refuge during a storm in 1773. Woodhouse drank the local wine which was very strong and decided to fortify it so it could be transported. He ended up staying in Marsala and supplying the British Navy with the wine. There is an amusing true story about Marsala wine. During the Prohibition period, bottles of Marsala, made by Florio in Sicily and destined for the USA, had 'Tonic' printed on their labels, with 'Dose: a small glassful twice a day'. Large bottles were labelled 'Hospital-size'.

1 X 1.5KG (3LB 5OZ) TURBOT
1 WINEGLASS DRY WHITE WINE
3 SPRIGS PARSLEY
SALT
BLACK PEPPERCORNS
PLAIN FLOUR
80G (SCANT 3OZ) BUTTER
½ WINEGLASS DRY MARSALA
1 TABLESPOON FINELY CHOPPED
  PARSLEY

Clean and fillet the fish, to give 4 fillets (or have the fish-monger do this for you). Reserve all the bones and trimmings from the fish, and put them in a saucepan with the wine, parsley sprigs, salt and a few peppercorns. Pour in 500ml (18floz) water. Simmer gently for 30 minutes, then strain the stock into another pan and reduce over a brisk heat for another 30 minutes.

Flour the fillets and fry them in butter until golden on both sides. Add the Marsala and half a wineglass of the reduced fish stock. Finish cooking over a strong heat to arrive at a smooth sauce. Sprinkle with the parsley and serve at once.

Brodetto in Bianco di Porto Recanati

FISH STEW FROM PORTO RECANATI

SERVES 4

Waverley Root writes in his book The Food of Italy *that brodetto was said to have been invented in Athens, and was spread throughout the Mediterranean by the Greeks. He writes that Julius Caesar consumed a similar version of this brodetto at Forum Livii (now Forli), before he crossed the Rubicon.*
Two thousand years later, Field Marshal Montgomery ate virtually the same dish at virtually the same spot. All along the Marche coast many types of brodetto are found.
Serve this with bruschetta – slices of Italian bread toasted on a griddle or ridged cast-iron grill pan, then rubbed with garlic, drizzled with extra virgin olive oil and sprinkled with salt.
'In bianco' means cooking without tomato.

- 1.2KG (2¾LB) ASSORTED FISH, SUCH AS WHITING, RED MULLET, GREY MULLET, MONKFISH
- 400G (14OZ) SQUID
- 2 CLOVES GARLIC, FINELY CHOPPED
- 2 TABLESPOONS FINELY CHOPPED PARSLEY
- 150ML (¼ PINT) EXTRA VIRGIN OLIVE OIL
- 175ML (6FLOZ) DRY WHITE WINE
- ½ WINEGLASS WHITE WINE VINEGAR
- A GOOD PINCH OF SAFFRON THREADS
- SALT AND FRESHLY GROUND BLACK PEPPER
- PLAIN FLOUR
- 4 MEDITERRANEAN PRAWNS
- 4 RAW SCAMPI (LANGOUSTINES)
- 8 CLAMS
- BRUSCHETTA, TO SERVE

For the stock
- 1 SMALL ONION, QUARTERED
- 4 SPRIGS PARSLEY
- 1 BAY LEAF

Wash and clean the fish, reserving the heads and trimmings. Cut the fish across into cutlets, to give 4 cutlets of each type. Make a strong stock from the fish heads and trimmings, onion, parsley sprigs, bay leaf and water to cover. Strain and keep hot.

Wash and skin the squid. Remove the ink sacs, eyes and mouths, and cut the bodies into rings. In a large two-handled shallow pan, briefly fry the garlic and chopped parsley in the olive oil. Add the squid bodies and tentacles. After a few minutes, add the wine and vinegar and boil to reduce rapidly. Cover with the hot stock and add the saffron and a seasoning of salt and pepper. Reduce the heat, cover the pan and cook for 15–20 minutes or until the squid are fairly tender.

Lightly flour the fish cutlets, and add to the pan together with the prawns and scampi. Cook over a relatively brisk heat, shaking the pan at regular intervals. Do not attempt to turn the fish. Add more stock if needed. Add the clams towards the end of cooking and, when they have opened, season the broth generously with salt and pepper. Serve the brodetto in large shallow soup bowls with bruschetta.

RIGHT *Brodetto in Bianco di Porto Recanati*

Pescatrice Impanata con Spinaci in Agrodolce

MONKFISH WITH SPINACH AND SWEET–SOUR SAUCE

SERVES **4**

Agrodolce means a combination of sweet and sour, a way of cooking which was much in vogue in the Ancient Roman and medieval periods.

Put the sultanas to soak in tepid water. Cut the monkfish into 4 portions and season with salt and pepper. Dip the fish into the beaten eggs and then roll in the breadcrumbs.

Heat a knob of the butter in a saucepan until foaming and cook the spinach until wilted and tender. Season with salt and add the drained sultanas and the pine nuts.

While the spinach is cooking, fry the fish in abundant hot olive oil until it is golden and crisp on both sides. In a small pan, make a sauce from the remaining butter, the sugar and vinegar.

Serve the fish with the sauce poured over and the spinach on one side.

50G (1¾ OZ) SULTANAS

400G (14OZ) BONELESS MONKFISH

SALT AND FRESHLY GROUND BLACK PEPPER

3 EGGS, LIGHTLY BEATEN

8 SLICES BREAD, CRUSTS REMOVED, MADE INTO BREADCRUMBS

200G (7OZ) SPINACH, WELL WASHED

75G (2½ OZ) BUTTER

20G (¾ OZ) PINE NUTS

EXTRA VIRGIN OLIVE OIL

I TABLESPOON SUGAR

2 TABLESPOONS RED WINE VINEGAR

ROMBO CON CHAMPIGNON

TURBOT WITH MUSHROOMS AND CLAMS

SERVES 4

Clams and cockles from the Mediterranean are much enjoyed by Italians, particularly in dishes such as the Neapolitan vermicelli or spaghetti 'alle vongole'. The same species of clam and cockle are found in British waters. 'Purging' the shellfish cleans them of sand.

700G (1LB 9OZ) CLAMS OR
  COCKLES
600G (1LB 5OZ) SKINNED TURBOT
  FILLET
8 SLICES PANCETTA
OLIVE OIL
150G (5½OZ) BUTTON
  MUSHROOMS, SLICED
A LARGE PINCH OF SAFFRON
  THREADS
4 TABLESPOONS SINGLE CREAM
SALT AND FRESHLY GROUND
  BLACK PEPPER

Wash the clams or cockles and purge, if necessary (see page 67). Cook them in a large frying pan, shaking the pan regularly, until all the shells are open. Take the clams or cockles from the shells and reserve. Filter the cooking liquid.

Cut the turbot into 8 pieces, and wrap a slice of pancetta round each piece. Fry the turbot in a little olive oil until golden. Remove and keep on one side. Fry the mushrooms in the same frying pan over a brisk heat. Add the clams or cockles with their cooking liquid, the saffron and cream and stir well. Return the turbot to the pan. Cover and cook for 3 minutes to reduce the sauce.

Season with salt and pepper and serve.

Coda di Rospo Arrosto con Salsa alle Alghe

Roasted monkfish with laverbread sauce and fried seaweed

SERVES 6

Laver is a smooth, fine seaweed found off the shores of South Wales. After thorough washing, the laver is boiled for about 6 hours until it is quite soft. The liquid is then drained off and the resulting mush is called laverbread. It is obtainable in wet fish shops in South Wales.

To prepare the deep-fried seaweed, wash the laver thoroughly – you will have to wash it many times to remove the sand, which adheres to it. Leave the seaweed to drain in a colander and then dry thoroughly. Tear the laver into strips. Deep fry until crisp, about 2–3 minutes. Sprinkle with a little freshly ground coriander. Set aside.

For the laverbread sauce, make a strong stock by simmering all the vegetables, herbs and peppercorns in the milk. Strain the stock, reserving half the potato, and pour into a blender or food processor. Add the reserved potato, the laverbread, cream and butter. Blend until smooth. Gradually mix in the orange juice – keep tasting, as more or less may be needed. The flavour of the sauce should be well balanced. Return the sauce to the pan and check the seasoning. Set aside.

Preheat the oven to 220°C/425°F/gas 7. Heat a veil of olive oil and a knob of butter in an ovenproof frying pan large enough to hold all the monkfish pieces. When the butter foams add the monkfish and fry until golden brown on both sides. Transfer the pan to the oven and cook for 4–5 minutes. (Be careful not to overcook the monkfish: the time in the oven will depend on the thickness of the fish.) While the monkfish is cooking in the oven, heat a veil of oil and a knob of butter in another pan and fry the scallops and prawns until just cooked. Keep warm. Heat the laverbread sauce to just below boiling.

Remove the monkfish from the oven. Put 3 tablespoons of laverbread sauce on each plate. Slice the monkfish pieces into two, cutting diagonally, and place the slices slightly overlapping on the sauce. Add the scallops and prawns, and surround with deep-fried laverbread and a few julienne of orange zest.

6 PIECES BONELESS MONKFISH, WEIGHING 175G (6OZ) EACH

6 SCALLOPS, CLEANED

6 RAW KING PRAWNS, PEELED

OLIVE OIL

BUTTER

SALT AND FRESHLY GROUND BLACK PEPPER

JULIENNE OF ORANGE ZEST, TO GARNISH

For the deep-fried seaweed

115G (4OZ) LAVER SEAWEED

VEGETABLE OIL FOR DEEP FRYING

CORIANDER SEEDS, GROUND

For the laverbread sauce

3 CARROTS, ROUGHLY CHOPPED

1 LEEK, ROUGHLY CHOPPED

1 ONION, ROUGHLY CHOPPED

2 STICKS CELERY, ROUGHLY CHOPPED

1 LARGE POTATO, WEIGHING ABOUT 225G (8OZ), QUARTERED

3 SPRIGS PARSLEY

2 BAY LEAVES

5 BLACK PEPPERCORNS

600ML (1 PINT) MILK

240ML (8FLOZ) LAVERBREAD

2 TABLESPOONS CREAM

3 KNOBS OF BUTTER

150ML (¼ PINT) FRESHLY SQUEEZED SEVILLE ORANGE JUICE, STRAINED

RIGHT *Coda di Rospo Arrosto con Salsa alle Alghe*

Rombo alla Diavola
Turbot with anchovy and paprika sauce

SERVES 4

Usually 'alla diavola' means cooked over hot coals, which has a relevance to Hell. In this case, it must be the red from the paprika which is associated with the devil.

Put the turbot in a deep dish and pour over half of the olive oil. Add the onion, garlic, cloves, thyme broken up, bay leaf, parsley, a few peppercorns and a pinch of salt. Leave to marinate at cool room temperature for at least 1 hour.

Mash the anchovies until smooth. Add the paprika and the remaining olive oil and mix to make a homogenous sauce.

Remove the fish from the marinade and dry on kitchen paper. Strain the marinade oil into a frying pan, heat and fry the fish.

Serve with the anchovy and paprika sauce poured over.

450G (1LB) TURBOT FILLET, CUT IN 4 PIECES

125ML (4FLOZ) EXTRA VIRGIN OLIVE OIL

1 MEDIUM ONION, FINELY CHOPPED

1 CLOVE GARLIC, ROUGHLY CHOPPED

5–6 CLOVES

1 SPRIG FRESH THYME

1 BAY LEAF, ROUGHLY TORN UP

2 SPRIGS PARSLEY

BLACK PEPPERCORNS

SALT

16 ANCHOVY FILLETS, DRAINED

½ TEASPOON PAPRIKA

Trote al Forno in Crosta di Speck
Baked trout with speck and savory

SERVES 4

Speck is smoke-cured ham flavoured with herbs and spices.

Preheat the oven to 200°C/400°F/gas 6. Season the trout with salt, pepper and thyme. Stuff the trout with savory and wrap each fish in 3 slices of speck.

Oil a baking tray and put the fish on it side by side. Drizzle with the sherry and some olive oil. Bake for 10 minutes. Serve hot.

4 TROUT, CLEANED

SALT AND FRESHLY GROUND BLACK PEPPER

DRIED THYME

1 BUNCH OF FRESH SAVORY

12 SLICES SPECK, CUT THINLY

2 TABLESPOONS DRY SHERRY

EXTRA VIRGIN OLIVE OIL

Merluzzo Grigliato al Coriandolo

GRILLED COD AND PEPPERS WITH CORIANDER SAUCE

SERVES 4

The combination of the orange-flavoured coriander and the lemon juice enhance the flavour of cod, which has a basically bland flavour.

Skin the peppers by holding them over a high gas flame to char the skins all over, or use a blowtorch to burn the skin off. Clean the peppers of any charred skin. Cut the peppers into thin slices, discarding all seeds, and toss the slices with the garlic, 1 tablespoon olive oil and a seasoning of salt. Set aside.

Preheat the grill. Score the skin once on each piece of cod. Season the fish with salt and pepper and drizzle over some olive oil. Grill the fish, skin side up first, until cooked.

In the meantime, put the coriander seeds, pepper, chervil, lemon juice and salt in a small saucepan and set over a low heat to warm. Gradually add the olive oil, mixing it in with a small balloon whisk as if making mayonnaise.

Make a bed of peppers on a platter, or on individual plates, put the fish on top and pour the sauce over the fish.

2 RED PEPPERS

2 YELLOW PEPPERS

1 CLOVE GARLIC, FINELY CHOPPED

EXTRA VIRGIN OLIVE OIL

SALT AND FRESHLY GROUND
  BLACK PEPPER

4 PIECES COD FILLET, WEIGHING
  800G (1¾LB) IN TOTAL

For the sauce

½ TABLESPOON CORIANDER
  SEEDS, CRUSHED

½ TABLESPOON COARSELY
  GROUND BLACK PEPPER

1 TABLESPOON CHOPPED FRESH
  CHERVIL

JUICE OF 1 LEMON

A PINCH OF SALT

100ML (3½FLOZ) EXTRA VIRGIN
  OLIVE OIL

Rombo con Rösti e Caponata Marchigiana

Turbot in a rösti crust with aubergine caponata

SERVES 4

*Do not cut basil with a knife as it discolours the leaves –
use your fingers for shredding.*

Cut the turbot or cod fillet into 4 equal pieces and set aside. Fry the pine nuts in 1 tablespoon of the olive oil until a light gold; drain on kitchen paper.

Cut the aubergines lengthways into quarters and remove the central flesh with seeds in it. Cut the remaining aubergine flesh, with the skin, into 1cm (½in) dice. Sprinkle the dice with salt and leave to drain in a colander for 30 minutes.

Peel the potatoes and shred them on a mandoline or, failing this, on a cheese grater. The result should be a matchstick effect. Do not put the potatoes in water as it would remove the starch.

Season the fish with salt and pepper. In a large non-stick frying pan, heat 75ml (2½ floz) of the olive oil. Divide half the shredded potato among the fish pieces, spreading it evenly on the top. When the oil is hot, put the fish in the pan, potato side down, using two fish slices. Fry until the potato crust is deep golden, then spread the remaining potato on top of the fish and turn the fish over. Cook until the bottom potato crust is deep golden. If the pieces of fish are thick, to ensure that the fish is cooked through, put the frying pan in a hot oven for about a minute.

While the fish is cooking, heat the remaining oil in another non-stick frying pan until smoking hot. Dry the aubergine dice, then add them to the oil and fry, stirring constantly, to seal them quickly. Add the tomato dice, pine nuts and shredded basil. Cook, stirring all the time, until the tomato is warmed through – about 1 minute. Taste for seasoning.

Divide the aubergine caponata among 4 plates, piling it up in a mound, and gently lay the fish on one side of the mound. Serve with a wedge of lemon.

800G (1¾LB) TURBOT OR COD
  FILLET
40G (1½OZ) PINE NUTS
160ML (5½FLOZ) EXTRA VIRGIN
  OLIVE OIL
400G (14OZ) AUBERGINES
600G (1LB 5OZ) POTATOES
SALT AND FRESHLY GROUND
  BLACK PEPPER
300G (10½OZ) TOMATOES, SKINNED,
  SEEDED AND CUT IN
  1CM (½IN) DICE
25 LARGE FRESH BASIL LEAVES,
  SHREDDED
1 LEMON, CUT IN 4 WEDGES

RIGHT *Rombo con Rösti e
Caponata Marchigiana*

Spigola con Carfiofi
e Barba di Frate

SEABASS WITH ARTICHOKES AND *BARBA DI FRATE*

Barba di frate *are the fresh young shoots of the salsify plant.*
If unobtainable, you can use spinach or samphire.

Cut each seabass fillet in half and score the skin of each piece twice. Mix together all the ingredients for the marinade in a shallow dish. Put in the pieces of seabass and leave to marinate at cool room temperature for about 1 hour.

Preheat the oven to 200°C/400°F/gas 6. Remove all the tough leaves from the artichokes and trim the tops. Cut each artichoke lengthways into 4 and remove any choke. As the artichokes are prepared, drop them into water with lemon juice added to it. Drain the artichokes and put them in a flameproof casserole with 2 tablespoons of the olive oil and a seasoning of salt and pepper. Cover the casserole with a tight-fitting lid. Bring to the boil, then transfer to the oven to cook for 30 minutes or until tender.

In the meantime, cook the *barba di frate* in boiling water until *al dente*. Drain and keep warm.

In a non-stick frying pan heat the remaining olive oil. Add the drained fish pieces, skin side down, and fry until the skin is crisp. Turn the fish pieces over, reduce the heat a little and fry until the fish is just cooked through. Remove the fish from the frying pan and keep warm. Add the marinade to the frying pan and cook for a minute or two, stirring.

Put the *barba di frate* in the centre of each plate and put two pieces of fish on the top. Surround with the artichoke wedges and pour the warmed marinade over the fish. Serve at once.

4 SEABASS FILLETS, WEIGHING 150G
(5½OZ) EACH

6 SMALL YOUNG GLOBE
ARTICHOKES (VIOLA TYPE)

LEMON JUICE

3 TABLESPOONS EXTRA VIRGIN
OLIVE OIL

SALT AND FRESHLY GROUND
BLACK PEPPER

200G (7OZ) *BARBA DI FRATE*

For the marinade

2 CLOVES GARLIC, FINELY
CHOPPED

30G (1OZ) PARSLEY, FINELY
CHOPPED

1 TABLESPOON FINELY CHOPPED
FRESH MARJORAM

1 TABLESPOON FINELY CHOPPED
FRESH THYME

JUICE OF 1 LEMON

1 WINEGLASS EXTRA VIRGIN
OLIVE OIL

Filetti di Muggine con Olive e Capperi

GREY MULLET FILLETS WITH OLIVE AND CAPER SAUCE

SERVES 4

Grey mullet tends to be an underrated fish. It has firm, flavoursome flesh and should be used more. As it feeds on organic material, it must be fished from unpolluted water.
The eggs of the grey mullet are used for Bottarga, *a Sardinian luxury. To make it, the eggs are salted, pressed together and then air dried.* Bottarga *is grated on pasta, or shaved on top of crostini and served with a drizzle of oil.*

Ask your fishmonger to clean, scale and fillet the grey mullet. You should be left with 4 fillets. Cut each fillet in half diagonally and score the skin on each piece 3 or 4 times.

Chop the celery and olives into small dice. Heat 6 tablespoons of the olive oil in a saucepan and add the garlic, celery and olives and heat through. Stir in the capers, tomatoes, thyme leaves and basil. Season with salt and pepper. Stir, then leave to cook on a very low heat for 10 minutes.

In the meantime, heat the remaining olive oil in a large non-stick frying pan and cook the mullet pieces, skin side down, for 3 minutes. Turn them and cook for a further 1 minute.

To serve, divide the olive and caper sauce among 4 plates and put the fish fillets on top. Drizzle with balsamic vinegar.

2 GREY MULLETS, WEIGHING 1.5KG (3LB 5OZ) IN TOTAL
7 TABLESPOONS EXTRA VIRGIN OLIVE OIL
12 SMALL CAPERS
2 PLUM TOMATOES, SKINNED, SEEDED AND DICED
SMALL WHITE HEART OF I BUNCH CELERY
6 BLACK OLIVES, STONED
4 GREEN OLIVES, STONED
I CLOVE GARLIC, FINELY CHOPPED
LEAVES FROM 4 SPRIGS FRESH THYME
2 FRESH BASIL LEAVES, TORN
SALT AND FRESHLY GROUND BLACK PEPPER
BALSAMIC VINEGAR

Involtini di Sgombri
Mackerel and mushrooms on skewers

Involtini *are small rolls or bundles, most often made from thin slices of veal or ham wrapped round a stuffing. Here the* involtini *are fresh mackerel fillets rolled round a seasoning of anchovies, capers and parsley.*

4 MACKEREL, WEIGHING 250G
  (9OZ) EACH
JUICE OF 1 LEMON
SALT AND FRESHLY GROUND
  BLACK PEPPER
4 ANCHOVY FILLETS PRESERVED
  IN OIL, DRAINED
1 TABLESPOON CAPERS PRESERVED
  IN VINEGAR, DRAINED
A HANDFUL OF PARSLEY, CHOPPED
FINE BREADCRUMBS MADE FROM
  2-DAY-OLD BREAD
EXTRA VIRGIN OLIVE OIL
8 BAY LEAVES
8 MUSHROOM CAPS
DRY WHITE WINE

Preheat the oven to 200°C/400°F/gas 6. Remove the head and fins from the mackerel, then fillet them. (A fishmonger will do this for you.) Put the fillets in a dish, skin side down, side by side. Season the fillets with the lemon juice, salt and pepper. Leave to marinate for 10 minutes, then drain.

Chop the anchovies and capers and mix with the parsley, 2 tablespoons breadcrumbs and 1 teaspoon olive oil. Divide among the mackerel and spread over the flesh. Roll the fillets up, from tail to head end. On to each of 4 wooden skewers thread a rolled mackerel fillet, a bay leaf, a mushroom cap, another rolled fillet, another mushroom and another bay leaf.

Roll the skewers in breadcrumbs and put on an oiled baking tray. Drizzle over dry white wine and olive oil. Bake for 20 minutes. Serve with some of the cooking juices.

Sarde in Porchetta

Sardines with Parma ham and herbs

SERVES **4**

'In porchetta' *means in the style of cooking roast pig.*

Preheat the oven to 180°C/350°F/gas 4. Remove the head and fins from the sardines, then scale and bone them. Be sure that you remove all the bones. Rinse the fishes in the white wine.

Fry the Parma ham and garlic in the olive oil until the garlic is light gold. Add the marjoram and fennel and cook gently for a few minutes. Add a splash of wine and reduce. Remove from the heat.

Cook the potatoes, in their skins, in boiling salted water. In the meantime, put the sardines, side by side, in a non-stick baking tin. Cover with the oil and herb mixture and season fairly generously with salt and pepper. Bake for 15 minutes.

Drain the potatoes. When cool enough to handle, peel and slice them. Serve the sardines with the warm sliced potatoes sprinkled with salt, pepper, vinegar and parsley.

16 SARDINES, WEIGHING 1 KG (2¼LB) IN TOTAL

100ML (3½FL OZ) DRY WHITE WINE

75G (2½OZ) FATTY PARMA HAM, THINLY SLICED, CUT IN JULIENNE

2 CLOVES GARLIC, FINELY CHOPPED

200ML (7FLOZ) EXTRA VIRGIN OLIVE OIL

2 TABLESPOONS FINELY CHOPPED FRESH MARJORAM

4 TABLESPOONS FINELY CHOPPED FRESH HERB FENNEL

SALT AND FRESHLY GROUND BLACK PEPPER

For the warm potato salad

800G (1¾LB) POTATOES

SALT AND FRESHLY GROUND BLACK PEPPER

WINE VINEGAR (PREFERABLY HOME-MADE)

FINELY CHOPPED PARSLEY

Tonno con Pepe alla Verdure Caramellate

SEARED PEPPERED TUNA WITH CARAMELIZED VEGETABLES

Tuna is a meaty fleshed fish, so pepper is a good accompaniment.
Nowadays fresh tuna is easily obtainable.

Put the sugar in a non-stick frying pan. Leave to melt and then caramelize over a strong heat. Add the vinegar, taking care as you do so (the sugar syrup will spit and sputter), and stir to mix with the caramel syrup. Allow the vinegar to evaporate a little, then add the water and 4 table-spoons olive oil. Bring to the boil, then remove from the heat and reserve.

In another non-stick frying pan heat the remaining 2 table-spoons olive oil. Add the garlic and all the vegetables and cook for a couple of minutes, tossing the vegetables. Add the caramel stock and reduce slightly. The vegetables should be *al dente*. Season with salt and pepper. Keep the vegetables warm.

Season each tuna slice with 1 teaspoon of cracked pepper and some salt. Heat a veil of olive oil in a non-stick frying pan until smoking hot. Sear the tuna on both sides. The tuna should be pink in the middle. To serve, cut each slice of tuna diagonally into two and slightly overlap on the plates. Serve with the caramelized vegetables and their juices.

4 SLICES TUNA, WEIGHING 170G (6OZ) EACH

4 TEASPOONS CRACKED BLACK PEPPER

SALT

EXTRA VIRGIN OLIVE OIL

For the caramelized vegetables

2 TABLESPOONS SUGAR

2 TABLESPOONS VINEGAR

1 WINEGLASS WATER

6 TABLESPOONS EXTRA VIRGIN OLIVE OIL

1 CLOVE GARLIC, FINELY CHOPPED

2 COURGETTES, CUT IN 1CM (½IN) DICE

1 AUBERGINE, CUT IN 1CM (½IN) DICE

16 SPRING ONIONS WITH 5CM (2IN) OF GREEN

½ RED PEPPER, CUT IN 1CM (½IN) DICE

½ YELLOW PEPPER, CUT IN 1CM (½IN) DICE

SALT AND FRESHLY GROUND BLACK PEPPER

MEAT DISHES

Petto d'Anitra ai Frutti di Montagna

DUCK BREASTS WITH WHIMBERRIES

SERVES 4

Whimberry is the Welsh name for bilberry.

Score the skin on the duck breasts in a grid pattern, being careful not to cut through to the flesh. Melt the butter in a non-stick frying pan and, when it foams, add the duck breasts, skin side down. Cook over a lively heat for 10 minutes, then turn and cook for another 10 minutes. Remove the breasts from the pan and leave to rest for 10 minutes, covered, with a weight on top.

Pour nearly all the fat from the frying pan, then return the breasts to the pan. Season with salt and pepper. Pour the cognac over the breasts and set alight. Remove from the heat for a few seconds until the flames have gone out. Return the pan to the heat and add the whimberries. Add the sugar and the vinegar and cook over a lively heat for 3–4 minutes, stirring frequently. Slice the duck breasts and serve with the berry sauce.

4 BONED DUCK BREASTS, WEIGHING ABOUT 160G (5¾OZ) EACH

20G (¾OZ) BUTTER

SALT AND FRESHLY GROUND BLACK PEPPER

2 TABLESPOONS COGNAC

150G (5½OZ) WHIMBERRIES OR BLUEBERRIES, WASHED AND DRIED

2 LEVEL TABLESPOONS SUGAR

3 TABLESPOONS VINEGAR

RIGHT *Petto d'Anitra ai Frutti di Montagna*

MEAT DISHES

Coniglio con Aceto Balsamico

RABBIT BRAISED IN BALSAMIC VINEGAR

SERVES 4

A purée of potatoes is good served with this rabbit dish.

Put the rabbit joints in a bowl and pour over the wine vinegar and cold water to cover. Leave to soak for 5 hours.

Rinse the rabbit thoroughly under cold running water. Dry the joints and put them in a flameproof casserole. Pour over the balsamic vinegar. Cover the casserole and let the balsamic vinegar slowly evaporate over a moderate heat. Add the butter, oil, stock, 1 tablespoon of the parsley and the garlic. Season with salt and pepper. Cover and cook gently for 45 minutes or until the rabbit is tender. If the rabbit is wild it will take longer – just keep on checking. Add more stock if necessary. When the rabbit is cooked, add the remaining parsley.

1 RABBIT, JOINTED

½ WINEGLASS WINE VINEGAR

1 WINEGLASS BALSAMIC VINEGAR

20G (¾OZ) BUTTER

2 TABLESPOONS EXTRA VIRGIN
  OLIVE OIL

125ML (4FLOZ) CHICKEN OR ANY
  LIGHT STOCK

2 TABLESPOONS FINELY CHOPPED
  FRESH FLAT-LEAF PARSLEY

1 CLOVE GARLIC, FINELY CHOPPED

SALT AND FRESHLY GROUND
  BLACK PEPPER

Noce di Cervo con Berberi

Noisettes of venison with barberries

Barberries have a tart flavour and are a beautiful red colour. They used to be found in the UK, but were practically exterminated when it was discovered they harboured wheat mildew parasites. If you are unable to find fresh barberries, you can use dried barberries – called zereshk, they can be purchased in Iranian shops. The dried barberries must be well washed before using and any stalks removed.

Bone the venison saddle. Keep the bones and scraps for stock, and cut the the meat into noisettes of about 100g (3½ oz) each. Mix together all the ingredients for the marinade and pour over the venison noisettes, making sure they are well covered – add more wine if needed. Leave the venison to marinate overnight, or up to 3 days if possible.

Preheat the oven to 200°C/400°F/gas 6. Put the bones and vegetables for the stock in a roasting tin and brown in the oven. Transfer the bones and vegetables to a large pan. Add a little water to the roasting tin and stir and scrape up the caramelized meat juices. Pour this liquid into the pan. Add the red wine (or 300ml/½ pint of the strained marinade) and the bouquet garni. Cover generously with water. Bring to the boil, then simmer gently, uncovered, for 3 hours. Skim regularly. Strain through a fine sieve. You should be left with about 300ml (½ pint) of rich stock.

Drain and dry the venison noisettes. Heat a little olive oil and butter in a frying pan and, when hot, fry the noisettes, searing and browning the outside well but not overcooking the interior. Season with salt and pepper. Transfer the noisettes to a warm serving dish and let them rest in a warm place for 5 minutes.

Add the cognac to the pan juices and stir to mix. Reduce until caramelized. Add the strained stock. Bring to the boil. Add the redcurrant jelly and stir until melted. Correct the seasoning, then strain the sauce into a saucepan. Add the barberries and heat through in the sauce. Pour over the noisettes and serve.

1 SADDLE OF VENISON, WEIGHING 2.25–2.7KG (5–6LB)

OLIVE OIL

BUTTER

SALT AND FRESHLY GROUND BLACK PEPPER

4 TABLESPOONS COGNAC

2 TABLESPOONS REDCURRANT JELLY

25G (SCANT 1OZ) DRIED BARBERRIES, WASHED, DRAINED AND STALKS REMOVED

For the marinade

1 LITRE (1¾ PINTS) RED WINE

4 JUNIPER BERRIES, LIGHTLY CRUSHED

2 SPRIGS FRESH THYME

2 BAY LEAVES

2 SPRIGS PARSLEY

2 CLOVES GARLIC, UNPEELED, CRUSHED

2 MEDIUM ONIONS, FINELY SLICED

2 CARROTS, FINELY SLICED

1 STICK CELERY, FINELY SLICED

4 TABLESPOONS OLIVE OIL

For the game stock

2 SMALL ONIONS, ROUGHLY CHOPPED

2 CARROTS, ROUGHLY CHOPPED

1 LARGE STICK CELERY, ROUGHLY CHOPPED

2 CLOVES GARLIC, PEELED

300ML (½ PINT) RED WINE

1 BOUQUET GARNI

AGNELLO IN SALSA ALL'AGLIO

LAMB CUTLETS WITH GARLIC SAUCE

SERVES 4

This recipe is best when both the garlic and the lamb are the new season's.

Trim the lamb cutlets of any excess fat. Mix together the ingredients for the marinade in a shallow dish. Add the cutlets and leave to marinate for 1 hour or so in a cool place, turning them over every now and then.

In the meantime, make the sauce. Preheat the oven to 200°C/400°F/gas 6. Wrap the whole garlic heads in aluminium foil and bake for 20 minutes. Cut the garlic heads across in half and squeeze out the pulp. Pass the pulp through a fine sieve, pushing it through with a spoon.

Melt the butter in a small pan over a very low heat. Add the garlic purée, a pinch of salt and the lemon juice and mix well together with a small whisk or wooden spoon. Remove the pan from the heat and slowly add the egg yolk as you would for a mayonnaise, whisking all the time. Keep the sauce warm in a covered bain-marie.

Heat the olive oil in a non-stick frying pan with 1 sprig of thyme and the bay leaves. Drain the lamb cutlets and put in the pan. Cook for 5 minutes on each side. Season with salt and pepper, then leave the cutlets to rest in the frying pan, off the heat, for about 3 minutes. Remove the cutlets and keep warm.

Reheat the frying pan, add the wine and boil to reduce to a glaze. Serve the cutlets with the garlic sauce poured on one side and some of the cooking juices drizzled round. Decorate with a few fresh thyme leaves scattered over.

12 LAMB CUTLETS

5 TABLESPOONS EXTRA VIRGIN OLIVE OIL

2 SPRIGS FRESH THYME

2 BAY LEAVES

SALT AND FRESHLY GROUND BLACK PEPPER

½ WINEGLASS WHITE WINE

For the marinade

½ WINEGLASS WINE VINEGAR

1 WINEGLASS DRY WHITE WINE

1 SPRIG FRESH ROSEMARY

¾ BLACK PEPPERCORNS

For the sauce

2 VERY LARGE HEADS GARLIC

60G (2OZ) BUTTER

JUICE OF ½ LEMON

1 EGG YOLK, LIGHTLY BEATEN

RIGHT *Agnello in Salsa all'Aglio*

Costolette d'Agnello all'Aceto Balsamico

LAMB CUTLETS WITH FRESH TOMATO, HERB AND BALSAMIC VINEGAR SAUCE

SERVES 4

This easy tomato and herb sauce is good with barbecued lamb chops, too. A rocket salad goes very well with them.

Mix the diced tomatoes with the herbs, garlic, olive oil and balsamic vinegar. Season with salt and pepper. Leave the sauce to macerate for at least 1 hour before using.

Trim the lamb cutlets of excess fat. Flatten the meat with a meat mallet or rolling pin between two pieces of cling film.

Heat a ridged cast-iron grill pan or griddle and cook the cutlets for a couple of minutes on each side. Season with salt and pepper. Serve with the sauce.

200G (7OZ) RIPE TOMATOES, SKINNED, SEEDED AND CHOPPED INTO SMALL DICE

1 TABLESPOON FRESH THYME LEAVES

2 TABLESPOONS FINELY CHOPPED PARSLEY

1 CLOVE GARLIC, FINELY CHOPPED

4 TABLESPOONS EXTRA VIRGIN OLIVE OIL

2 TABLESPOONS BALSAMIC VINEGAR

SALT AND FRESHLY GROUND BLACK PEPPER

12 LAMB CUTLETS

Polpette di Agnello

Lamb rissoles

SERVES 4

A recipe common in the Marche region of Italy. The polpette *are served here with* Salsa del Papa, *or Pope's sauce. It is not really known why the sauce has this name. What is known is that the sauce was in very common usage throughout the Pontificate state and was always served with fried cutlets. It was often found on Marchigiani hotel menus of the period. Instead of* Salsa del Papa, *olives fried in olive oil with garlic and grated orange zest can be used and are equally delicious.*

Mix the lamb with the lemon juice, beaten egg, breadcrumbs, pecorino, cinnamon, parsley, and a seasoning of salt and pepper. Divide into 8 equal balls and gently flatten to discs about 1.5cm (⅝in) thick. Dust each disc with flour, dip in the beaten eggs and then roll in the breadcrumbs which have been mixed with the grated lemon zest, coating evenly all over.

Heat the olive oil with the butter in a frying pan and fry the *polpette* until golden brown on both sides and cooked through. Drain on kitchen paper.

In the meantime, make the sauce. Fry the onion in a knob of butter with the olive oil until soft. Add the water and boil to reduce by one-third. Stir in the olives, capers and vinegar. Finally, add the anchovy fillets mashed with a knob of butter.

Serve the *polpette* with the sauce.

450G (1LB) MINCED LAMB

2 TABLESPOONS LEMON JUICE

1 EGG, LIGHTLY BEATEN

30G (1OZ) FRESH BREADCRUMBS

3 TABLESPOONS FRESHLY GRATED
PECORINO OR PARMESAN

2 GENEROUS PINCHES OF GROUND
CINNAMON

1 TABLESPOON FINELY CHOPPED
FRESH FLAT-LEAF PARSLEY

SALT AND FRESHLY GROUND
BLACK PEPPER

2 TABLESPOONS OLIVE OIL

A KNOB OF BUTTER

For coating

PLAIN FLOUR

2 EGGS, LIGHTLY BEATEN

65G (2¼OZ) FINE FRESH
BREADCRUMBS

GRATED ZEST OF ½ LEMON

For the sauce

4 TABLESPOONS FINELY CHOPPED
ONION

2 KNOBS OF BUTTER

1 TABLESPOON OLIVE OIL

240ML (8FLOZ) WATER

100G (3½OZ) SMALL BLACK
OLIVES, STONED

2 TABLESPOONS SMALL CAPERS
PRESERVED IN VINEGAR,
DRAINED

1 TABLESPOON WINE VINEGAR

4 ANCHOVY FILLETS

STINCO D'AGNELLO CON ROSMARINO

LAMB SHANKS WITH ROSEMARY

SERVES 4

Preheat the oven to 190°C/375°F/gas 5. Trim any excess bone and sinews from the lamb shanks. Fry them in 2 tablespoons of the olive oil until lightly browned all over. Place the shanks in a heavy, deep, preferably cast-iron casserole with the cooking oil. Add the rosemary, garlic and wine and season with salt and pepper. Cover the casserole tightly and cook in the oven for 1½–2 hours or until tender. After cooking for an hour check the sauce; if it is drying out too much add some water.

When the lamb shanks are cooked remove them from the casserole and pat dry with kitchen paper. Put them in a roasting tin, bone end standing up. Increase the oven heat to 200°C/400°F/gas 6. Brush the shanks with beaten egg and cover with a mixture of the breadcrumbs and Parmesan. Drizzle with the remaining olive oil. Put the roasting tin in the oven and bake until the breadcrumbs are golden.

Meanwhile, sieve the sauce and skim off the fat. Reduce the sauce to a pouring consistency. Serve the shanks with the sauce poured around, garnished with rosemary.

8 LAMB SHANKS (FRONT LEG)

4 TABLESPOONS EXTRA VIRGIN
   OLIVE OIL

8 SMALL SPRIGS FRESH ROSEMARY
   PLUS EXTRA TO GARNISH

32 CLOVES GARLIC, PEELED

2 WINEGLASSES DRY WHITE WINE

SALT AND FRESHLY GROUND
   BLACK PEPPER

2 EGGS, LIGHTLY BEATEN

6 TABLESPOONS FRESH
   BREADCRUMBS

4 TABLESPOONS FRESHLY GRATED
   PARMESAN

RIGHT *Stinco d'Agnello*
con Rosmarino

Fegato d'Agnello
all'Aceto Balsamico
SAUTÉED LAMB'S LIVER WITH BALSAMIC VINEGAR

Serve with Cipolle Bianche all'Aceto Balsamico *(see page 123).*

Remove the skin from the liver and slice into 5mm (¼in) thick slices. Remove any tubes with a very sharp knife. Lightly beat the eggs on a plate and season with salt and pepper. Dip the slices of liver in flour and then in the egg and then coat with the breadcrumbs.

Melt the butter in a frying pan and, when it is foaming, add the liver slices. Fry until golden on both sides. Remove the slices from the frying pan and sprinkle with balsamic vinegar. Serve at once.

300G (10½ OZ) LAMB'S LIVER

2 EGGS

SALT AND FRESHLY GROUND
BLACK PEPPER

2 TABLESPOONS PLAIN FLOUR

FINE DRY BREADCRUMBS

50G (1¾ OZ) BUTTER

BALSAMIC VINEGAR

Maiale ai Capperi
PORK MEDALLIONS WITH CAPERS

SERVES 4

The combination of capers and balsamic vinegar cuts the richness of the pork.

Heat the oil in a non-stick frying pan and fry the pork medallions to sear on each side. Season with salt and pepper. Reduce the heat and cook for a further 2 minutes. Remove the pork from the frying pan and keep warm.

Add the sugar and balsamic vinegar to the pan and stir with a wooden spoon until the sugar is dissolved. Add the capers and cook for 1 minute. Serve the pork with the sauce poured over.

450G (1LB) PORK TENDERLOIN
(FILLET), CUT INTO 4 MEDALLIONS

4 TABLESPOONS EXTRA VIRGIN
OLIVE OIL

SALT AND FRESHLY GROUND
BLACK PEPPER

1 LEVEL TEASPOON SUGAR

2 TABLESPOONS BALSAMIC
VINEGAR

2 TABLESPOONS SALTED CAPERS,
WELL RINSED

MAIALE CON MORTELLA DI PALUDE
PORK MEDALLIONS WITH CRANBERRIES

SERVES **4**

*In the UK, dried cranberries can be found in most supermarkets
all year round. Everyone thinks that cranberries are American,
but in fact they are found in many parts of Europe too.
This sauce can be used with chicken as well.*

In a small saucepan mix together the sugar and cornflour
and stir in the wine and stock until smooth. Add the
balsamic vinegar, cranberries, tarragon and a seasoning of salt
and pepper. Simmer for 15 minutes, stirring occasionally. Stir
in the chopped parsley and cook for 1 more minute. Keep
the sauce warm.

Heat the oil in a non-stick frying pan and fry the pork
medallions for 2 minutes on each side. Season with salt and
pepper. Reduce the heat and cook for a further 2 minutes.

Serve the pork medallions with the sauce poured round.

1 X 450G (1LB) PORK TENDERLOIN
(FILLET), CUT IN 4 MEDALLIONS

4 TABLESPOONS EXTRA VIRGIN
OLIVE OIL

For the sauce

50G (1¾OZ) DEMERARA SUGAR

1 TABLESPOON CORNFLOUR

240ML (8FLOZ) WINE

125ML (4FLOZ) CHICKEN STOCK

1 TEASPOON BALSAMIC VINEGAR

70G (2½OZ) DRIED CRANBERRIES

A PINCH OF DRIED TARRAGON,
CRUMBLED

SALT AND FRESHLY GROUND
BLACK PEPPER

2 TEASPOONS FINELY CHOPPED
FRESH FLAT-LEAF PARSLEY

Costarelle in Porchetta con Patate

SPARE RIBS WITH POTATOES IN TOMATO-HERB SAUCE

SERVES 4

This recipe is very common in the Marche. It is a cheap and tasty dish.

In a shallow flameproof casserole, fry the spare ribs in 2 tablespoons of olive oil until golden. Add the garlic and fry briefly. Season the spare ribs generously with salt and pepper. Add the wine and cook briskly until the wine has evaporated. Add the tomatoes and herbs and pour in enough hot water to cover. Cover the casserole and cook gently for 1¼ hours or until the spare ribs are tender. Turn the spare ribs regularly.

About 20 minutes before the end of cooking, fry the potatoes in the remaining olive oil until golden. Season with salt and add to the spare ribs to finish cooking. If the sauce has reduced too much, add more water. The sauce should coat the ribs and be quite dense. Skim off any excess fat before serving.

1KG (2¼LB) SHORT SPARE RIBS

4 TABLESPOONS EXTRA VIRGIN OLIVE OIL

4 CLOVES GARLIC, FINELY CHOPPED

SALT AND FRESHLY GROUND BLACK PEPPER

2 WINEGLASSES DRY WHITE WINE

750G (1LB 10OZ) PLUM TOMATOES, SKINNED, SEEDED AND DICED

30G (1OZ) FRESH HERB FENNEL FRONDS, FINELY CHOPPED

6 SPRIGS FRESH ROSEMARY

1KG (2¼LB) EGG-SIZED POTATOES, PEELED AND CUT IN HALF LENGTHWISE

Tournedos con Salsa al Formaggio

Fillet steaks with cheese sauce

SERVES 4

Both Gruyère and fontina melt beautifully, which is what makes them ideal cheeses for smooth unctuous sauces as well as fondue (fontina is used for the Piedmontese fonduta, *which is served with sliced white truffles).*

Encircle each fillet steak with a slice of speck and tie with a piece of string to hold it firmly. Cut the remaining 2 slices of speck into strips and fry in a little olive oil; reserve. Heat a veil of olive oil in a frying pan and fry the steaks medium, turning once. Season with salt and pepper.

Meanwhile, prepare the sauce by gently heating the cream and stirring in the two cheeses. Season with salt and pepper. Keep warm. In a small frying pan, quickly toss the spring onions in a little hot olive oil.

Divide the sauce among 4 plates. Place the steak in the centre and garnish with the julienne of speck and the spring onions.

4 FILLET STEAKS, WEIGHING 150G
(5½ OZ) EACH

6 SLICES SPECK

EXTRA VIRGIN OLIVE OIL

SALT AND FRESHLY GROUND
BLACK PEPPER

8 SPRING ONIONS, WHITE PART
ONLY, CUT DIAGONALLY IN 3CM
(1¼ IN) LENGTHS

For the sauce

200ML (7FLOZ) SINGLE CREAM

100G (3½ OZ) GRUYÈRE,
GRATED

100G (3½ OZ) FONTINA,
GRATED

FETTINA DEL CURATO

SIRLOIN STEAK WITH HERB AND ANCHOVY SAUCE

SERVES 4

Christian tradition has two stories about basil: one that it grew in the container in which Salome put John the Baptist's head; the other that the Empress Helena, mother of the Roman Emperor Constantine, found it growing on the spot of Christ's Crucifixion. An accompaniment of new potatoes is all that is necessary for this dish.

Put all the sauce ingredients into a blender or food processor and blend until smooth.

Beat the steaks with a meat mallet until quite thin. Heat the olive oil in a large frying pan, or 2 medium ones, and when very hot add the steaks. Season with salt and pepper and sear on both sides. Remove the steaks from the frying pan and keep warm.

Pour the sauce into the pan. Remove the pan from the heat and swirl the sauce so that it is warmed through. Pour the sauce over the steaks and serve.

4 SIRLOIN STEAKS, TRIMMED OF FAT

4 TABLESPOONS EXTRA VIRGIN OLIVE OIL

SALT AND FRESHLY GROUND BLACK PEPPER

For the sauce

1 BUNCH OF FRESH BASIL (ABOUT 36 LARGE LEAVES)

1 TABLESPOON FINELY CHOPPED FRESH MARJORAM

5 CLOVES GARLIC

¼ SMALL ONION, FINELY CHOPPED

1 SPRIG FRESH ROSEMARY, FINELY CHOPPED

A PINCH OF MUSTARD POWDER

8 ANCHOVY FILLETS PRESERVED IN OIL, DRAINED

JUICE OF 4 LEMONS

5 TEASPOONS WHITE WINE VINEGAR

VEGETABLES

Melanzane Imbottite di Bucatini e Mozzarella

Aubergines stuffed with bucatini and mozzarella

SERVES 4

This recipe is based on an idea from a restaurant in Palermo, called Charleston. Use the round, light purple variety of aubergine, known as Tunisino, for this dish.

Slice the stalk end off each aubergine to make a lid; reserve. Scoop out the flesh from the aubergines, leaving 1cm (½in) of flesh all round. Chop the scooped-out flesh into small cubes. Deep fry the aubergine 'bowls' and the lids until tender (put the frying basket on top to keep the aubergines immersed in the oil). Remove and put to drain on kitchen paper. To keep their shape, hang the 'bowls' upside down over glasses.

Preheat the oven to 200°C/400°F/gas 6. In a saucepan, fry the shallots and garlic in 4 tablespoons of the olive oil until golden. Add the aubergine dice and fry until golden. Add the tomato dice, with any juice, and the tomato passata. Season with salt, pepper and oregano. Cook until the sauce has thickened.

Cook the pasta in abundant boiling lightly salted water until *al dente*. Drain and put in a bowl. Add the torn basil leaves, mozzarella and half the tomato sauce. Mix in well.

Put the remaining tomato sauce in a gratin dish that will hold all the aubergines. Fill the aubergine 'bowls' with the pasta mixture and set them upright in the dish. Drizzle the remaining olive oil on top and sprinkle with the Parmesan. Bake for 20 minutes. Serve at once, with the lids on the top for decoration.

4 AUBERGINES, WEIGHING ABOUT
1.3KG (3LB) IN TOTAL

OLIVE OIL FOR DEEP FRYING

2 SHALLOTS, FINELY CHOPPED

2 CLOVES GARLIC, FINELY
CHOPPED

5 TABLESPOONS EXTRA VIRGIN
OLIVE OIL

1KG (2¼LB) TOMATOES,
SKINNED, SEEDED AND DICED,
ANY JUICE RESERVED

4 TABLESPOONS TOMATO PASSATA

SALT AND FRESHLY GROUND
BLACK PEPPER

A GENEROUS PINCH OF DRIED
OREGANO

250G (9OZ) BUCATINI

20 FRESH BASIL LEAVES, TORN

300G (10½OZ) MOZZARELLA,
DICED

20G (¾OZ) PARMESAN, FRESHLY
GRATED

RIGHT *Melanzane Imbottite di Bucatini e Mozzarella*

Zucchini al Forno con Parmigiano e Prosciutto

BAKED COURGETTES WITH PARMESAN AND PARMA HAM

SERVES 4-6

Preheat the oven to 200°C/400°F/gas 6. Oil a baking tin that measures about 33 x 23 x 5cm (13 x 9 x 2in).

Cook the whole courgettes in boiling water for about 5 minutes. Drain. Top and tail the courgettes, and cut each lengthways in 4. Wrap each quarter in a slice of Parma ham and arrange side by side in the tin. Sprinkle with the Parmesan and season with pepper.

Bake for 10 minutes or until lightly browned. Serve hot.

3 SMALL COURGETTES, WEIGHING
   ABOUT 450G (1LB) IN TOTAL
100G (3½OZ) THINLY SLICED
   PARMA HAM
25G (SCANT 1OZ) PARMESAN,
   FRESHLY GRATED
FRESHLY GROUND BLACK PEPPER
OLIVE OIL

Pomodori Verdi Fritti

FRIED GREEN TOMATOES

SERVES 6

This is a clever way of using unripened tomatoes. The dish is a good accompaniment to either grilled meat or fish.

Slice the tomatoes. Mix chilli powder and salt to taste into the breadcrumbs. Dip the slices of tomato into the beaten eggs, then coat with breadcrumbs. Heat some olive oil in a frying pan and fry the tomatoes until golden and crisp on both sides. Drain on kitchen paper and serve hot.

1KG (2¼LB) GREEN TOMATOES
CHILLI POWDER
SALT
FINE DRY BREADCRUMBS
2 EGGS, LIGHTLY BEATEN
OLIVE OIL

Welsh Bubble and Squeak

SERVES **4**

Young wild garlic leaves can be used in salads, or chopped and then sprinkled on top of new potatoes. They can also be added to mayonnaise, after being finely chopped.

900G (2LB) POTATOES SUITABLE
   FOR MASHING

50G (1¾OZ) WILD GARLIC
   LEAVES, WASHED AND COARSELY
   CHOPPED

BUTTER

115G (4OZ) STREAKY BACON,
   FINELY CHOPPED

10–15 FRESH MINT LEAVES,
   CHOPPED

SALT AND FRESHLY GROUND
   BLACK PEPPER

PLAIN FLOUR

OLIVE OIL

Cook the potatoes, in their skins, in boiling salted water. Drain in a colander. When they are cool enough to handle, peel them. Pass them immediately through a potato ricer or mouli-légumes to make a fine purée.

In a covered frying pan, sweat the wild garlic leaves with 2 knobs of butter. Add a little water and continue cooking un-covered until the leaves are tender and the water evaporated.

In another frying pan, fry the bacon until crisp; discard nearly all the fat. Add the bacon and remaining fat to the potato purée, together with the wild garlic leaves, mint and a seasoning of salt and pepper. Fold all the ingredients together. Shape into a cylinder about 5cm (2in) in diameter on a well-floured board. Cut across into 2.5cm (1in) thick rounds and flour them well.

Heat some olive oil and butter in a frying pan. When the butter starts to foam, add the potato cakes and fry until brown and crisp on both sides. Serve hot.

Insalata di Pomodoro con Insavurida
Tomato salad

SERVES **4**

All the ingredients for the insavurida
(dialect for insaporita, *meaning very tasty) must be chopped
so finely they are almost emulsified.*

Mix together the herbs, onion and garlic and add the olive oil and balsamic vinegar. Season with salt and pepper and mix well together. Thinly slice the tomatoes and dress with the *insavurida*.

1 TABLESPOON VERY FINELY
  CHOPPED PARSLEY
½ TABLESPOON VERY FINELY
  CHOPPED FRESH BASIL
1 TABLESPOON VERY FINELY
  CHOPPED ONION
½ CLOVE GARLIC, VERY FINELY
  CHOPPED
3 TABLESPOONS EXTRA VIRGIN
  OLIVE OIL
1 TABLESPOON BALSAMIC VINEGAR
SALT AND FRESHLY GROUND
  BLACK PEPPER
4 MEDIUM ITALIAN SALAD
  TOMATOES (MARMANDE)

Fichi Fritti
Deep-fried figs

SERVES **6**

*Figs done in this way come from the Naples area, where years
ago they were a street snack. They are also prepared like this in the
Marche, when there is a glut of figs (which invariably there
is, in season).*

Drop the figs in boiling water for a second, then drain. Make a cross in the stalk end, cutting straight down but not all the way through. Lightly beat the eggs with a pinch of salt. Dip the figs in flour and then in the egg, then coat with breadcrumbs. Deep fry the figs until they are golden all over. Drain on kitchen paper and serve at once.

18 SMALL FIRM FIGS
3 EGGS
SALT
PLAIN FLOUR
FINE DRY BREADCRUMBS
OLIVE OIL FOR DEEP FRYING

RIGHT *Fichi Fritti*

V E G E T A B L E S

Pizzelle di Melanzane
Aubergine pizza–style

*Salted capers need to be rinsed before use, to remove the salt.
Put them in a sieve and hold under running cold water.*

Season the tomato dice with salt and pepper, and add the oregano, a little olive oil and the capers. Mix together, then leave to marinate for at least 3 hours.

Without peeling, slice the aubergines into 12 slices, each 1.5cm (⅝in) thick. Season the slices with salt. Fry briefly in a little hot olive oil until golden on both sides. Place the slices on kitchen paper and place another piece of kitchen paper on top. Press lightly to drain them of excess oil.

Preheat the grill. Spread the aubergine slices on a baking tray. Divide the tomato mixture among them. Sprinkle over the diced mozzarella, then add the olive halves and a little salt and pepper. Grill until the mozzarella has just melted. Serve at once.

400G (14OZ) TOMATOES,
  SKINNED, SEEDED AND CUT INTO
  SMALL DICE
SALT AND FRESHLY GROUND
  BLACK PEPPER
A GOOD PINCH OF DRIED
  OREGANO
EXTRA VIRGIN OLIVE OIL
20G (¾OZ) SALTED CAPERS,
  WELL RINSED
600G (1LB 5OZ) AUBERGINES
  (PREFERABLY THE ROUND
  VARIETY)
200G (7OZ) MOZZARELLA, DICED
12 BLACK OLIVES, STONED AND
  HALVED

Barba di Frate all'Aglio

Barba di frate with garlic and chilli

SERVES 4

Barba di frate, *or roscani as it is known in the Marche, are the young shoots of the salsify plant. The young plants are pulled up and sold in bunches during the early spring. Keen gardeners should grow this vegetable as it is delicious. Never cover* barba di frate *when cooking or it will go black.*

400G (14OZ) *BARBA DI FRATE*

SALT

2 TABLESPOONS EXTRA VIRGIN OLIVE OIL

2 CLOVES GARLIC, FINELY CHOPPED

1 FRESH RED CHILLI, SEEDED AND FINELY CHOPPED

1 LEMON, CUT IN 4 WEDGES

Remove the woody part from the *barba di frate*, and wash thoroughly to remove all the soil. Steam or boil the *barba di frate* for 5 minutes, then season with salt. Heat the olive oil in a frying pan and stir in the garlic and chilli. Add the *barba di frate* and toss in the oil for about 5 minutes or until tender. Serve hot, with the lemon wedges to squeeze over.

An alternative, simpler way of preparing *barba di frate* is to cook it in boiling lightly salted water for 10 minutes. Drain, then season with salt and pepper and dress with extra virgin olive oil and lemon juice to taste.

FRITTEDDA

BRAISED SPRING VEGETABLES

SERVES 4

Prepare the artichokes by removing the hard outer leaves and trimming off the stalk, leaving about 5cm (2in) attached to the artichoke. Peel the stalk and trim round the base of the artichoke. Cut off the tips of the artichoke leaves straight across with a sharp knife. Cut each artichoke lengthways into 5 segments and drop into water acidulated with lemon juice.

Shell the broad beans and peas. If there are any large beans among the broad beans, always remove the outer skins.

Fry the onion in the olive oil in a saucepan until light gold. Add the artichoke segments, well drained. Stir them well into the onion and oil mixture, then add a ladle of water. Add the beans and peas to the pan. Season with salt, pepper and a little grating of nutmeg. Leave to cook over a low heat, stirring occasionally and adding a little more water if necessary.

When the artichokes are tender, add the wine, sugar and mint. Mix well and cook for a further 2–3 minutes. Serve either hot or cold.

6 TENDER PURPLE GLOBE
 ARTICHOKES (VIOLA OR SPINOSI)
LEMON JUICE
1KG (2¼LB) FRESH YOUNG
 BROAD BEANS
500G (1 LB 2OZ) FRESH PEAS
1 SMALL ONION, FINELY CHOPPED
3 TABLESPOONS EXTRA VIRGIN
 OLIVE OIL
SALT AND FRESHLY GROUND
 BLACK PEPPER
FRESHLY GRATED NUTMEG
3 TABLESPOONS DRY WHITE WINE
½ TEASPOON SUGAR
12 FRESH MINT LEAVES, CHOPPED

RIGHT *Frittedda*

CRUCCHÉ DI PATATE E RICOTTA

POTATO AND RICOTTA CROQUETTES WITH CINNAMON

MAKES 10

Cook the potatoes, in their skins, in boiling salted water until tender, then drain. Or cook them in a microwave oven. When the potatoes are cool enough to handle, peel them and pass them through a potato ricer or mouli-légumes to make a fine purée. Lightly beat the 2 egg yolks and add to the potato purée with half of the breadcrumbs and the Parmesan. Mix well. Season with salt and pepper. Form the potato mixture into 10 balls.

Mix the ricotta with the cinnamon. Divide the ricotta mixture into 10, and stuff each potato ball with a portion of the ricotta mixture. Lightly beat the egg whites until frothy. Dip each potato ball in beaten egg white, then coat in the remaining breadcrumbs. Deep fry the ricotta *crucché* in hot olive oil until golden brown all over. Drain on kitchen paper and serve hot, lightly salted.

1KG (2¼LB) POTATOES

2 EGGS, SEPARATED

100G (3½OZ) FINE
BREADCRUMBS

25G (SCANT 1OZ) PARMESAN,
FRESHLY GRATED

SALT AND FRESHLY GROUND
BLACK PEPPER

500G (1LB 2OZ) RICOTTA

25G (SCANT 1OZ) GROUND
CINNAMON

OLIVE OIL FOR DEEP FRYING

TEGLIETE GRATINATE
GRATIN OF COURGETTES AND TOMATOES

SERVES 4

This can be eaten on its own as a first course, or as an accompaniment to a main dish.

Preheat the oven to 220°C/425°F/gas 7. Top and tail the courgettes, then thinly slice them lengthways. Alternate the slices of courgette and tomato in a flower pattern in 4 gratin dishes. Mix the breadcrumbs with the thyme, marjoram, 2 tablespoons of olive oil and a seasoning of salt and pepper. Cover the vegetables with the breadcrumb mixture and drizzle over a little olive oil. Bake for about 10 to 15 minutes until a golden crust has formed on the top. Serve these vegetables tepid.

400G (14OZ) COURGETTES

300G (10½ OZ) TOMATOES, CORED AND SLICED

6 SLICES BREAD, WITHOUT CRUST, MADE INTO COARSE BREADCRUMBS

½ TABLESPOON FINELY CHOPPED FRESH THYME

½ TABLESPOON FINELY CHOPPED FRESH MARJORAM

EXTRA VIRGIN OLIVE OIL

SALT AND FRESHLY GROUND BLACK PEPPER

POMODORI GRATINATI
BAKED STUFFED TOMATOES

SERVES 4

This tomato dish can also be cooked on a barbecue. Place the tomatoes on a mesh cooling rack before putting them over the hot coals.

Cut the tomatoes in half and remove the central flesh and seeds with a teaspoon. Sprinkle the insides of the tomato halves with salt and put them, cut side down, in a colander. Leave them to drain for 20 minutes.

Preheat the oven to 170°C/325°F/gas 3. Oil a baking tray. Mix the parsley, garlic, breadcumbs, oregano, capers and salt together. Stuff each tomato half with this mixture and place the tomatoes, side by side, in the baking tray. Drizzle a little oil over the tomatoes. Bake for about 30 minutes or until the surface of the tomatoes is golden. Serve tepid.

4 MEDIUM-SIZE FIRM, RIPE TOMATOES

PINCH OF SALT

I TABLESPOON FINELY CHOPPED FRESH FLAT-LEAF PARSLEY

I CLOVE GARLIC, FINELY CHOPPED

3 TABLESPOONS FRESH BREADCRUMBS

A PINCH OF DRIED OREGANO

2 TABLESPOONS SMALL SALTED CAPERS, WELL RINSED AND CHOPPED

EXTRA VIRGIN OLIVE OIL

Zucca all'Agrodolce

Pumpkin in sweet and sour sauce

SERVES 4

Pumpkin is much enjoyed in Italy, in soups and risotto, as well as to make a stuffing for ravioli.

Cut the pumpkin in half, discard all seeds and fibres, and peel off the skin. Cut the flesh in 1cm (½in) thick slices. Heat the olive oil in a frying pan and fry the pumpkin slices until tender and golden brown on both sides. Season with salt and pepper. Transfer the pumpkin to a serving dish.

Pour half of the oil from the pan, then return the frying pan to the heat and add the wine vinegar and sugar. Stir with a wooden spoon until the sugar is dissolved. Pour the vinegar and sugar syrup over the pumpkin. Sprinkle the mint and garlic over the pumpkin. Serve cold.

750G (1LB 10OZ) YELLOW PUMPKIN

3 TABLESPOONS EXTRA VIRGIN OLIVE OIL

SALT AND FRESHLY GROUND BLACK PEPPER

1 WINEGLASS WHITE WINE VINEGAR

1 TEASPOON SUGAR

8 FRESH MINT LEAVES OR MORE TO TASTE, FINELY CHOPPED

2 CLOVES GARLIC, FINELY CHOPPED

RIGHT *Zucca all'Agrodolce*

POMODORI FRITTI IN CARPIONE
MARINATED FRIED TOMATOES

MAKES **10 CROQUETTES**

Cut the tomatoes into slices 4mm (scant ¼ in) thick. Beat the eggs with a fork and season with salt. Lightly flour the tomato slices, then dip in the beaten egg and coat with breadcrumbs. Fry the breadcrumbed tomato slices, a few at a time, in abundant hot olive oil until crisp and golden brown on both sides. Remove with a perforated spoon and drain on kitchen paper.

When all the tomato slices have been fried, discard nearly all the oil. In the remaining oil fry 1 tablespoon of bread-crumbs until golden. Add the tomato paste, sugar, lemon juice, vinegar, capers and a ladle of water and stir well. Leave to simmer for 5 minutes, then pour the mixture over the tomatoes which have been put in a serving dish. These tomatoes can be served at once or left to marinate for a couple of hours before serving.

4 LARGE TOMATOES, SKINNED

2 EGGS

SALT

PLAIN FLOUR

FINE DRY BREADCRUMBS

EXTRA VIRGIN OLIVE OIL

½ TEASPOON TOMATO PASTE

1 TEASPOON SUGAR

JUICE OF 1 LEMON

2 TABLESPOONS RED WINE
VINEGAR

50G (1¾OZ) SMALL SALTED
CAPERS, WELL RINSED

CIME DI RAPE
TURNIP TOPS

SERVES **4-6**

Ideally turnip tops should only be used when they are very young.

Cut off any stalks from the turnip tops which seem a bit hard. Wash the tops thoroughly. The tops can either be steamed until tender or just cooked in the water left on them after washing.

Heat the olive oil in a frying pan, add the anchovy fillets and garlic, and stir with a wooden spoon until the anchovies are broken up. Add the turnip tops and toss into the mixture. Add the parsley and season with salt and pepper, then toss again. Serve hot or cold.

1KG (2¼LB) TURNIP TOPS

3 TABLESPOONS EXTRA VIRGIN
OLIVE OIL

6 ANCHOVY FILLETS PRESERVED IN
OIL, DRAINED

1 CLOVE GARLIC, FINELY CHOPPED

1 TABLESPOON FINELY CHOPPED
FRESH FLAT-LEAF PARSLEY

SALT AND FRESHLY GROUND
BLACK PEPPER

Cipolle Bianche all'Aceto Balsamico

White onions in balsamic marinade

These onions can be kept 2–3 days.

Cut the tops off the onions and remove the thin outer skin and roots. Rinse and dry the onions well.

In a large frying pan heat the olive oil and gently cook the onions over a low heat until they are tender and translucent but not golden. Turn the onions gently with a wooden spoon during cooking. When the onions are ready, pour half of the oil from the pan. Season the onions with salt and pepper and add the sugar. Using either a wooden spoon or spatula, turn the onions over in the dissolved sugar to caramelize them, being careful not to burn the caramel. Place the caramelized onions in a bowl and leave to get cold.

Cover the onions with the oil and balsamic vinegar marinade and leave for an hour or more. Serve cold or reheat and serve hot.

1KG (2¼LB) SMALL YOUNG WHITE ONIONS

3 TABLESPOONS EXTRA VIRGIN OLIVE OIL

SALT AND FRESHLY GROUND BLACK PEPPER

2 TABLESPOONS CASTER SUGAR

For the marinade

500ML (18FLOZ) EXTRA VIRGIN OLIVE OIL

120ML (4FLOZ) BALSAMIC VINEGAR

Porri al Prosciutto
Impanati e Fritti
Wine-poached leeks wrapped in parma ham

SERVES **6**

These leeks served with Glamorgan Sausages (see page 14) and cockle fritters make an interesting Welsh-style fritto misto. To make cockle fritters, add cooked cockles to a basic fish batter to which finely chopped spring onions, salt and a generous amount of freshly ground rough pepper has been added. Deep fry a tablespoon at a time until golden. Drain on kitchen paper and serve.

3 LARGE LEEKS, WEIGHING ABOUT
  800G (1¾LB) IN TOTAL
BUTTER
SALT AND FRESHLY GROUND
  BLACK PEPPER
4 TABLESPOONS DRY WHITE WINE
6 SLICES PARMA HAM, WEIGHING
  150G (5½OZ) IN TOTAL
2 EGGS, BEATEN
6 SLICES BREAD, CRUSTS
  REMOVED, MADE INTO
  BREADCRUMBS
120ML (4FLOZ) EXTRA VIRGIN
  OLIVE OIL

Preheat the oven to 200°C/400°F/gas 6. Trim the leeks, removing all the tough leaves. Clean the leeks thoroughly under running cold water. Cut them in half lengthways and lay them in a gratin dish. Dot with flakes of butter, season with salt and pepper and pour over the wine. Cover the dish with aluminium foil. Bake for 20 minutes or until the leeks are just tender but still firm (*al dente*). Leave to cool.

When the leeks are cold, drain them and pat dry with kitchen paper. Wrap each one in a slice of Parma ham. Dip into the beaten eggs, then roll in the breadcrumbs to coat. Make sure the leeks are completely covered in breadcrumbs.

Heat the olive oil in a frying pan and fry the leeks over a moderate heat until they are crisp and golden brown on all sides. Drain on kitchen paper and serve at once.

SWEETS

Ricotta Fritta
Fried ricotta balls

MAKES **30**

These ricotta balls are good served on their own or with vanilla ice cream.

Mix together the ricotta, crushed amaretti, 2 of the eggs and the cinnamon. Form the mixture into balls the size of golf balls. Lightly beat the remaining 2 eggs. Roll the balls first in beaten egg and then coat in breadcrumbs. Fry the balls, a few at a time, in hot oil until golden brown all over. Remove the balls with a perforated spoon and drain on kitchen paper. Serve dusted with icing sugar.

400G (14OZ) RICOTTA

200G (7OZ) AMARETTI BISCUITS, CRUSHED

4 EGGS

2 PINCHES OF GROUND CINNAMON

150G (5½OZ) FINE DRY BREADCRUMBS

LIGHT OIL FOR DEEP FRYING

ICING SUGAR

Panettone Perdu

SERVES **4**

Here pain perdu, or eggy bread, is made with panettone, the sweet and spicy Italian bread full of sultanas and candied fruit.

Break the eggs into a flat dish. Add the cold milk and sugar and beat together well with a fork. Soak the slices of panettone in the egg mixture, pricking each slice with a fork here and there.

Melt the butter in a non-stick frying pan. Put the slices of panettone into the foaming butter and cook until both sides are golden. Drain, sprinkle with icing sugar and serve.

4 EGGS

175ML (6FLOZ) COLD MILK

4 TABLESPOONS ICING SUGAR, SIFTED, PLUS MORE FOR SPRINKLING

8 SLICES PANETTONE

40G (1½OZ) BUTTER

PANE DORATO
FRIED MASCARPONE SANDWICHES

SERVES 4

Pane Dorato *are given to children, and to those who are not so young, for* merenda — *elevenses.*

Soak the sultanas in hot water for a few minutes, then drain and dry thoroughly. Spread the mascarpone on each slice of bread. On four slices of bread sprinkle the sultanas and demerara sugar. Place the other 4 slices of bread on top, mascarpone side down, and press lightly together. Cut off the crusts and cut into triangular sandwiches.

Beat the eggs with the cream in a large flat bowl. Heat the butter in a non-stick frying pan. Dip the sandwiches one at a time in the egg mixture, impregnating the bread well on both sides, then fry the sandwiches in the hot butter until golden brown, about 3–4 minutes on each side. Serve hot, sprinkled with caster sugar.

4 TABLESPOONS SULTANAS

100G (3½OZ) MASCARPONE

8 THIN SLICES BREAD

4 TABLESPOONS DEMERARA SUGAR

2 EGGS

4 TABLESPOONS SINGLE CREAM

75G (2½OZ) BUTTER

CASTER SUGAR FOR SPRINKLING

FERRATELLE
WAFFLES

MAKES APPROX. 20

The waffle irons used for making ferratelle *in Italy often have a family crest on them, so each waffle is marked with the crest.*

Sift the flour into a bowl. Add the eggs, and mix in a little olive oil and a little liqueur to make a smooth soft paste. Shape into little rolls the size of a finger or into small apricot-sized balls.

Heat a waffle iron. Place a roll or a ball of paste on the iron, close up the iron and cook over a moderate heat on both sides until the waffle is amber in colour. Serve hot or cold.

300G (10½OZ) PLAIN FLOUR

3 EGGS

OLIVE OIL

ANISE LIQUEUR

Ferratelle della Trebbiatura
Lemon waffles

MAKES 20

After a few goes you will find that it is quite easy to get the hang of making these. In Italy, they are served either with caffè corretto, espresso coffee with anise (an aniseed liqueur), or with a glass of wine during the harvesting season.

Mix together all the ingredients and knead into an elastic compact paste.

Heat a waffle iron. Put a piece of paste the size of a walnut on the waffle iron, close it and cook over a moderate heat for a few minutes on each side. The waffles should be golden brown. Remove the waffles from the iron with the tip of a knife. Serve hot or cold.

4 EGGS

4 TABLESPOONS CASTER SUGAR

4 TABLESPOONS EXTRA VIRGIN OLIVE OIL

225G (8OZ) PLAIN FLOUR

GRATED ZEST OF 1 LEMON

A PINCH OF FENNEL SEEDS (OPTIONAL)

RIGHT *Ferratelle della Trebbiatura*

Fiori di Zucchini Dolci
Sweet fried courgette flowers

Use male flowers, which are the ones with just a stalk (female flowers are attached to a large base that bulges and resembles a baby courgette, which is what it is).

Wash and dry the courgette flowers. Remove the stamens. Mix together the ricotta, chocolate, rum, coffee and sugar to a creamy consistency. Divide the mixture among the courgette flowers. Gently squeeze the petals together just above the filling.

Dust the flowers first in flour, then dip them in beaten egg and, finally, coat with breadcrumbs. A light hand must be used for this exercise so that you do not crush the delicate flowers.

Deep fry the flowers in hot oil until golden all over. Drain on kitchen paper. Dust the flowers with cocoa powder and icing sugar and serve at once.

4 LARGE COURGETTE FLOWERS

100G (3½ OZ) FRESH RICOTTA

15G (½ OZ) BITTER CHOCOLATE, GRATED

1½ TABLESPOONS DARK RUM

3 TABLESPOONS ESPRESSO COFFEE

2 TEASPOONS CASTER SUGAR

PLAIN FLOUR

1 EGG, BEATEN

FINE DRY BREADCRUMBS

LIGHT VEGETABLE OIL FOR DEEP FRYING

COCOA POWDER

ICING SUGAR

CREMA BRUCIATA DI CAFFÈ

COFFEE CRÈME BRÛLÉE

SERVES 8

Preheat the oven to 170°C/325°F/gas 3. In a bowl whisk together the whole egg, egg yolks and sugar. Heat the cream and milk in a heavy saucepan until just boiling. Add the espresso coffee powder and liqueur and stir until the powder is dissolved. Pour the cream mixture into the egg mixture in a stream, whisking constantly. Skim off any froth.

Divide the custard among 8 ramekins or heatproof cups and set them in a baking tray. Pour enough hot water into the tray to reach half way up the sides of the ramekins. Bake the custards in the middle of the oven for about 40 minutes or until just set and trembling. Leave the custards to cool, then chill for at least 4 hours.

Cover the tops of the custards with an even layer of brown sugar and caramelize with a blowtorch.

1 LARGE EGG PLUS 6 LARGE EGG YOLKS

120G (4OZ) GRANULATED SUGAR

400ML (14FLOZ) DOUBLE CREAM

400ML (14FLOZ) MILK

1½ TABLESPOONS INSTANT ESPRESSO COFFEE POWDER

2 TABLESPOONS TIA MARIA OR KAHLUA

45G (1½OZ) SOFT LIGHT BROWN SUGAR

GELATO DI LAMPONI E YOGOURT

RASPBERRY AND YOGURT ICE

SERVES 6-8

This ice 'cream' is fine for people who cannot eat eggs.
It is a very refreshing ice.

Purée the raspberries in a blender or food processor, then pass them through a fine non-metallic sieve to remove the pips. Add half of the sugar and the Kirsch to the raspberry purée.

In a bowl, combine the yogurt, remaining sugar and milk. Beat together with a balloon whisk. Add the raspberry purée and mix in well. Freeze the mixture in an ice cream machine according to the manufacturer's instructions.

500G (1LB 2OZ) RASPBERRIES

120G (4OZ) CASTER SUGAR

1 TABLESPOON KIRSCH

200G (7OZ) PLAIN FULL-CREAM YOGURT

4 TABLESPOONS MILK

Panna Cotta al Caffè
Coffee-flavoured mascarpone custard

SERVES 4–6

Put half the sugar, the lemon juice and 4 tablespoons water into a heavy-based saucepan and dissolve over a low heat, stirring every now and then. Do not allow the water to boil before the sugar has dissolved.

In the meantime, heat 4–6 ramekins in a warm oven.

When the syrup is quite clear, bring it to a gentle boil and, without stirring, let it turn a golden colour. Be careful it does not burn. Remove the ramekins from the oven and pour in the caramel, tipping the dishes to coat the sides and bottom completely. Be careful as you are dealing with very hot caramel. Set the dishes aside.

In the saucepan in which the caramel was cooked, combine the mascarpone, milk, coffee powder and remaining sugar. Bring the mixture slowly to the boil, whisking with a balloon whisk to break up the mascarpone. Remove the pan from the heat and leave the mixture to cool and infuse for 1 hour.

In a cup, soften the gelatine in 4 tablespoons of water. Set the cup in a pan of hot water and stir until the gelatine is completely dissolved and clear. Stir briskly into the mascarpone mixture. Pour the mixture into the caramel-coated ramekins and refrigerate until firm. To serve, invert each ramekin onto a plate and shake the *panna cotta* loose. If you like, decorate with coffee beans.

170G (6OZ) CASTER SUGAR

JUICE OF ½ LEMON

225G (8OZ) MASCARPONE

400ML (14FLOZ) MILK

2 TEASPOONS INSTANT ESPRESSO
  COFFEE POWDER

10G (SCANT ⅓OZ) POWDERED
  GELATINE

COFFEE BEANS, TO DECORATE
  (OPTIONAL)

RIGHT *Trio of Coffee:*
Crema Bruciata di Caffè (see page
131); Panna Cotta al Caffè;
Gelato al Caffè (see page 139)

Pangelato alla Marchigiana

Coffee ice cream cake

SERVES **8–10**

This is based on a recipe from a periodical published in 1932 called Terra Picena. *Rosolio is a pink, rose-flavoured liqueur. If unobtainable you can use Strega instead.*

Preheat the oven to 180°C/350°F/gas 4. Prepare the mixture for the *pan di spagna* (see page 135) and pour into a buttered 21 x 10 x 6cm (8½ x 4 x 2½in) loaf tin. Bake in the centre of the oven for 20–25 minutes or until the cake feels springy to the touch and has come slightly away from the sides of the tin. Leave to cool in the tin for 3 minutes before tipping onto a sheet of greaseproof paper sprinkled with a little caster sugar.

For the filling, boil the coffee until reduced to 1 tablespoon. Beat the egg yolks with the sugar and butter until smooth and fluffy. Add the reduced coffee a little at a time, beating constantly.

Slice the *pan di spagna* into 4 horizontally. Drizzle each slice with Rosolio. Line the loaf tin in which the cake was baked with cling film, leaving some hanging over the sides. Place a layer of liqueur-moistened cake in the bottom of the tin and spread with a third of the egg and coffee mixture. Carry on layering until the cake and egg mixture are used up, finishing with cake. Fold the cling film over the top. Chill the cake in the freezer for 3 hours. Serve directly from the freezer, cut in slices.

For the pan di spagna

3 EGGS, SEPARATED

85G (3OZ) CASTER SUGAR

85G (3OZ) PLAIN FLOUR

½ TEASPOON BAKING POWDER

For the filling

120ML (4FLOZ) ESPRESSO COFFEE

8 EGG YOLKS

4 TABLESPOONS CASTER SUGAR

140G (5OZ) BUTTER, SOFTENED

4 TABLESPOONS ROSOLIO

Pan di Spagna

Plain sponge cake

Preheat the oven to 180°C/350°F/gas 4. Grease a swiss roll tin that measures 22.5 x 7.5 x 7.5cm (9 x 3 x 3in) and line it with greased greaseproof paper.

Whisk the egg yolks with the sugar until the mixture is fluffy. In another bowl, with a clean dry whisk, whisk the whites until stiff. Sift the flour with the baking powder. Using a metal spoon, fold the egg whites into the egg and sugar mixture, alternating with the sifted flour and baking powder. Spoon the mixture into the prepared swiss roll tin.

Bake for 10 minutes. Leave the cake to cool in the tin for 5 minutes before turning out on to a wire rack.

2 EGGS, SEPARATED

45G (1½OZ) CASTER SUGAR

45G (1½OZ) PLAIN FLOUR

¼ TEASPOON BAKING POWDER

Salsa di Caffè

Coffee sauce

Serve this with a trio of coffee-flavoured desserts: Crema Bruciata di Caffè (page 131), Panna Cotta al Caffè (page 132) and Gelato al Caffè (page 139).

Mix the milk with the coffee powder, then heat until boiling. In a bowl beat the egg yolks and sugar together until light and creamy. Pour the heated milk on to the egg mixture, stirring all the time. Return the sauce to a clean saucepan and cook over a gentle heat, stirring, until thickened.

300ML (½ PINT) MILK

3 TEASPOONS INSTANT ESPRESSO COFFEE POWDER

3 EGG YOLKS

60G (2OZ) CASTER SUGAR

CASSATA ABRUZZESE
NOUGAT AND CHOCOLATE CAKE

Torrone is a delicious Italian nougat. Both it and almond croccante can be found in Italian delicatessens. You might also look for Centerbe there, which is a herb-flavoured liqueur that is supposed to be made from 100 herbs, all gathered from around the massive peaks of the Maiella in Abruzzo.

Chop separately the *torrone*, *croccante* and chocolate. Beat the softened butter until it is light and fluffy. Beat in the egg yolks one at a time, alternating with the icing sugar. Divide this cream into 3 equal parts. Add the *torrone* to one part, *croccante* to the second part and the chocolate and cocoa powder to the third part. Mix each of the creams thoroughly.

In a bowl mix together 1 heaped tablespoon of each cream and reserve. Divide the *pan di spagna* into 4 equal discs. Drizzle the liqueur lightly over each disc to moisten. Spread one disc with *torrone* cream, a second disc with *croccante* cream and a third disc with chocolate cream. Layer them up, putting the fourth disc on top. Cover the whole of the cake with the mixed cream mixture. Leave the cake in the fridge for at least 6 hours before serving.

100G (3½OZ) *TORRONE*

50G (1¾OZ) ALMOND
    CROCCANTE (BRITTLE)

1 X 50G (1¾OZ) BLOCK GOOD
    PLAIN CHOCOLATE

300G (10½OZ) BUTTER,
    SOFTENED AND CUT INTO PIECES

6 EGG YOLKS

200G (7OZ) ICING SUGAR, SIFTED

50G (1¾OZ) COCOA POWDER

400G (14OZ) *PAN DI SPAGNA*
    (SEE PAGE 135), BAKED IN A ROUND
    TIN

200ML (7FLOZ) CENTERBE
    LIQUEUR (SWEET)

RIGHT *Cassata Abruzzese*

Semifreddo Maddalene
Iced mascarpone and amaretti dessert

SERVES 6–8

Semifreddi *are frozen sweets made either with cream,
mascarpone or confectioner's custard, with other ingredients,
such as fruit, crumbled biscuits or fruit syrups, added.*

Beat the egg yolks with the sugar until light and creamy.
Add the mascarpone and mix in well. Fold in the
candied fruit, chopped chocolate and crumbled amaretti.
Whisk the egg whites until stiff and fold into the mascarpone
mixture.

Line a loaf tin with cling film. Cover the sides and bottom
with slices of *pan di spagna* that have been drizzled with dry
Marsala. Fill the tin with the mascarpone mixture. Cover
with the remaining slices of Marsala-drizzled *pan di spagna*.
Cover the tin with cling film and freeze for 3–4 hours. Serve
sliced.

2 EGGS, SEPARATED
100G (3½OZ) CASTER SUGAR
200G (7OZ) MASCARPONE
100G (3½OZ) CANDIED FRUIT PEEL,
  FINELY DICED
100G (3½OZ) GOOD DARK
  CHOCOLATE, FINELY CHOPPED
150G (5½OZ) AMARETTI
  BISCUITS, CRUMBLED
PAN DI SPAGNA (SEE PAGE 135),
  THINLY SLICED
DRY MARSALA

Mattonella allo Zabaione e Fragole
Frozen zabaione and strawberry terrine

SERVES 6

This is another semifreddo. *It is basically strawberries and cream.*

Put the strawberries, half of the sugar and the wine in a
blender or food processor and blend until smooth. Pour
the strawberry purée into an oblong freezerproof mould
(such as a loaf tin or terrine).

Whisk the egg yolks with the remaining sugar until thick
and pale. Whip the cream until soft peaks form, then fold into
the egg mixture. Pour on top of the strawberry purée in the
mould. Freeze for at least 3 hours or until firm.

Serve the *mattonella* sliced and decorated with mint leaves
and slices of strawberry.

400G (14OZ) RIPE STRAWBERRIES
200G (7OZ) CASTER SUGAR
½ WINEGLASS SWEET RED WINE,
  SUCH AS VERNACCIA
4 EGG YOLKS
250ML (9FLOZ) WHIPPING CREAM
To decorate
FRESH MINT LEAVES
STRAWBERRIES

Gelato al Caffè
Coffee ice cream

SERVES 6

Serve this ice cream with Panna Cotta al Caffè (see page 132) and Crema Bruciata di Caffè (see page 131) as part of a trio of coffee desserts. A little coffee sauce (see page 135) is the finishing touch.

5 EGG YOLKS

200G (7OZ) CASTER SUGAR

350ML (12FLOZ) MILK

3 TABLESPOONS ESPRESSO COFFEE

Whisk the egg yolks and sugar in a large bowl until creamy. Bring the milk to the boil in a heavy saucepan, and gradually pour it on to the egg mixture. Stir in the coffee. Return the mixture to the saucepan and place over a moderate heat. Stir with a wooden spoon until the mixture thickens enough to coat the back of the spoon. Remove from the heat and cool quickly, then freeze in an ice cream machine according to the manufacturer's instructions.

Gelato di Miele e Armagnac
Honey and armagnac ice cream

MAKES 2 LITRES (3½ PTS)

This is a very soft and very rich ice cream.

6 EGGS, SEPARATED

300ML (½ PINT) CLEAR HONEY

150ML (¼ PINT) ARMAGNAC

600ML (1 PINT) DOUBLE CREAM
(PREFERABLY JERSEY CREAM),
WHIPPED

225G (8OZ) ICING SUGAR

Beat the egg yolks until they are thick and pale. Whisk the egg whites until they are stiff, then fold into the egg yolks. Mix the remaining ingredients together and fold into the egg mixture. Pour into a freezerproof container and freeze for 4–5 hours.

WHIMBERRY SORBET

In Wales, bilberries are known as whimberries. They grow in profusion on the Black Mountains and other surrounding mountains around Abergavenny. They are a wonderfully flavoured tiny purple fruit, with a grey bloom, which grow on low dense bushes. Back-breaking to pick but worth every effort.

115G (4OZ) SUGAR

150ML (¼ PINT) WATER

450G (1LB) WHIMBERRIES

JUICE OF ½ LEMON

To serve

DOUBLE CREAM OR VODKA

WHIMBERRIES

FRESH MINT LEAVES

Make a syrup by boiling the sugar and water together for 5 minutes. Allow to cool.

Sieve the whimberries, and add the cooled syrup and lemon juice to the resulting purée. Stir well. Pour the mixture into an ice cream machine and churn for 5 minutes.

Serve with double cream, or pour a little vodka over the sorbet, and decorate with whole whimberries and sugared mint leaves.

To sugar the mint leaves, paint them lightly with beaten egg white, dip them in caster sugar, shake off the excess sugar and leave them to dry in a warm place.

Torta di Formaggio al Limone

Lemon cheese cake

SERVES **8**

This is based on a recipe from Robert Carrier, which we first tried 34 years ago. It has been a constant favourite of Martyn Lewis, the newscaster, whom we often welcome at The Walnut Tree Inn.

Preheat the oven to 130°C/250°F/gas ½. To make the biscuit base, crush the biscuits in a polythene bag using a rolling pin. Mix the biscuits with the melted butter. Press the biscuit mixture on to the bottom of a 21cm (8½ in) loose-bottomed square cake tin. Bake for 5 minutes. Leave the base to get cold.

Beat the cream cheese, mascarpone, sugar, lemon zest and juice, vanilla essence and egg yolks together with an electric mixer until the mixture is smooth and creamy.

Meanwhile, in a cup, soften the gelatine in a little water. Set the cup in a small saucepan of hot water and stir until the gelatine is completely dissolved and clear. Remove the cup from the pan and leave the gelatine to cool to room temperature.

Whip the cream until soft peaks form. Whisk the egg whites until stiff but not dry. Fold the cream into the cheese mixture, then fold in the egg whites followed by the gelatine. Pour the mixture into the tin. Chill for at least 2 hours or until the filling has set.

400G (14OZ) LIGHT PHILADELPHIA CREAM CHEESE

200G (7OZ) MASCARPONE

135G (SCANT 5OZ) CASTER SUGAR

GRATED ZEST AND JUICE OF 1 LARGE LEMON

2 TEASPOONS VANILLA ESSENCE

4 EGGS, SEPARATED

15G (½OZ) POWDERED GELATINE

250ML (9FLOZ) WHIPPING CREAM

For the biscuit base

8 PLAIN CHOCOLATE DIGESTIVE BISCUITS

25G (SCANT 1OZ) BUTTER, MELTED

Pizza di Ricotta

Ricotta and chocolate 'pizza'

SERVES 12–14

This 'pizza' is very popular in Italian households and is usually served with sparkling wine when friends pop in.

First make the dough. Sprinkle the yeast into the flour, then rub in the butter. Add the whole eggs and egg yolks and work together into a smooth dough. Leave to rest for 30 minutes, covered with a cloth.

To make the filling, beat the sieved ricotta and sugar together until smooth. Fold in the remaining ingredients. Set aside.

Roll out two-thirds of the pastry dough and use to line a 22cm (8½ in) loose-bottomed flan tin. Leave to rest in the fridge for 30 minutes. Keep the remaining dough covered.

Preheat the oven to 200°C/400°F/gas 6. Fill the pastry case with the ricotta mixture. Make a lattice on top using the remaining pastry dough. Brush with egg wash. Bake for 30 minutes. Leave the 'pizza' in the tin until cooled. Serve at room temperature.

For the dough

A PINCH OF DRIED YEAST

500G (1LB 2OZ) PLAIN FLOUR

100G (3½ OZ) BUTTER

2 WHOLE EGGS PLUS 2 EGG YOLKS

1 EGG BEATEN WITH A FEW DROPS OF WATER, FOR EGG WASH

For the filling

500G (1LB 2OZ) RICOTTA, SIEVED

300G (10½ OZ) CASTER SUGAR

4 EGG YOLKS

FINELY GRATED ZEST OF 1 LEMON

30G (1OZ) CHOPPED MIXED CANDIED PEEL

A PINCH OF GROUND CINNAMON

30G (1OZ) GOOD PLAIN CHOCOLATE, GRATED

3 TABLESPOONS DARK RUM

Torta della Nonna
Lemon and strega tart

SERVES **8**

Lievito di vaniglia, *which is a vanilla-flavoured baking powder, is available in Italian delicatessens.*

First make the pastry dough. Mix the flour, salt, sugar, eggs and liqueur together in a bowl. Add the butter and *lievito di vaniglia*, mixing well. Leave the dough to rest in the fridge for 30 minutes, covered with cling film.

In the meantime, make the filling. Combine all the ingredients in the top of a double boiler over hot water, or in a pan or heatproof bowl set in a bain marie, and whisk until the mixture thickens like a curd. Remove from the hot water and leave to cool.

Preheat the oven to 180°C/350°F/gas 4. Divide the dough in 2 portions, one slightly larger than the other. Roll out into 2 circles. Use the larger circle to line a well-buttered 20cm (8in) loose-bottomed flan tin. Add the filling and cover with the other circle of dough. Press the edges together to seal. Brush the lid with the egg wash and sprinkle with the pine nuts. Bake for 40 minutes.

Remove the *torta* from the oven and place on a wire cooling rack. When the *torta* is tepid, sift icing sugar over it. Serve cold.

For the pastry dough
300G (10½ OZ) PLAIN FLOUR
A PINCH OF SALT
150G (5½ OZ) CASTER SUGAR
2 SMALL EGGS
2 LIQUEUR GLASSES OF STREGA LIQUEUR
80G (SCANT 3OZ) BUTTER
1 PACKET (16G) *LIEVITO DI VANIGLIA*

For the filling
9 EGGS
265ML (9½ FLOZ) DOUBLE CREAM
350G (12OZ) SUGAR
GRATED ZEST AND JUICE OF 5 LEMONS

To finish
1 WHOLE EGG PLUS 2 EGG YOLKS, BEATEN WITH A PINCH OF SALT, FOR EGG WASH
2 TABLESPOONS PINE NUTS
ICING SUGAR

Bacio

CHOCOLATE AND HAZELNUT KISSES

MAKES ABOUT **100**

Melt the sugar in a heavy pan, then cook the resulting syrup to a caramel. Add the hazelnuts and stir in quickly, then turn on to an oiled stainless steel tray. Leave to get cold. When cold and set, crush the caramelized nuts until they are the size of nibbed almonds.

Bring the cream to the boil. Add the milk chocolate off the heat and stir until smooth. Add the crushed caramelized nuts and stir in. Pour the mixture into a stainless steel tin and leave to get cold. When the mixture is cold place in the freezer to set hard.

With a 2.5cm (1in) parisienne scoop or melon baller, make balls from the mixture. Into each ball press a whole hazelnut, then dip into melted bitter chocolate to coat. When set keep these chocolates refrigerated.

150G (5½OZ) GRANULATED
 SUGAR
150G (5½OZ) SKINNED
 TOASTED HAZELNUTS
400ML (14FLOZ) DOUBLE CREAM
720G (1LB 9½OZ) MILK CHOCOLATE,
 FINELY CHOPPED
ABOUT 100 WHOLE HAZELNUTS
MELTED BITTER CHOCOLATE FOR
 DIPPING

BREADS

CIABATTA

ITALIAN SLIPPER BREAD

MAKES **3** LOAVES

This recipe was given us by a young baker from Recanati, in the Marche. Recanati was the home town of the great nineteenth-century Italian poet Giacomo Leopardi.

1KG (2¼LB) STRONG PLAIN FLOUR

1KG (2¼LB) VERY COLD WATER

10G (GENEROUS ¼OZ) FRESH YEAST

25G (SCANT 1OZ) SALT

Put the flour and half the water in an electric mixer. Mix well with the dough hook until a stiff dough is obtained. Slowly add the rest of the water a little at a time. Add the yeast and salt towards the end. Put the dough in an oiled bowl and leave to rise until trebled in size. Divide the dough with a pastry scraper into 3 (it will be very sloppy). Place each portion on a floured tray, stretching it into a long flat loaf as you do so. Try to handle as little as possible. Leave to prove for 20 minutes. Preheat the oven to 230°C/450°F/gas 8. Bake for 30 minutes or until golden brown.

CRESCIA DI MONTEFELTRO

POLENTA FLAT BREADS

MAKES **12**

Montefeltro was a small territory which was part of the Dukedom of Urbino between the thirteenth and the beginning of the sixteenth century.

500G (1LB 2OZ) COOKED
  POLENTA (SEE PAGE 60), COOLED

150G (5½OZ) PLAIN FLOUR

EXTRA VIRGIN OLIVE OIL

1 TABLESPOON LARD

Mash the polenta with a potato masher. Add the flour and 2 tablespoons of olive oil and knead together until homogenous. Make into 12 balls. Roll out each ball with a rolling pin and spread a little lard and olive oil on the surface, then roll up and reshape into a ball again. Roll out once more to a disc about the size and thickness of a pancake, and prick with a fork here and there.

Heat a griddle over a moderate heat. Cook the *crescia* until golden brown on both sides. Sprinkle with salt and serve.

BREADS

Calzone all'Andriese

Folded stuffed pizza

SERVES 8–10

Calzone *originated in Puglia, but radiated all over Italy. According to Luigi Sade, a scholar of Pugliese gastronomy,* calzone *appears for the first time in* 'Statuti' di Bisceglia, calzuni et similia, *written in the fifteenth century.*

S ift the flour and salt into a bowl. Make a hollow in the flour. Cream the yeast with a little tepid water and pour into the hollow with the olive oil. Mix together, adding sufficient water to bind to a standard bread dough consistency. Leave the dough to rise in a draught-free place for about 1½ hours.

To make the filling, lightly brown the spring onions in the olive oil. Keep the heat low so that the onions do not burn. Add the anchovies, olives, capers, tomatoes and sultanas. Cook over a high heat for a few minutes, stirring constantly so that the mixture does not catch. Season with salt and pepper, then remove from the heat and add the cheese.

Preheat the oven to 220°C/425°F/gas 7. Divide the dough into 2, one piece slightly larger than the other. Roll out the larger portion and use to line an oiled round flat tin 35cm (14in) in diameter. The dough should slightly overlap the sides. Add the filling and spread evenly. Roll out the remaining dough to make a lid. Fold the overlapping dough up over the lid and pinch the edges together to seal. Prick the top with a fork in numerous places. Brush with olive oil. Bake for 1 hour.

Allow the *calzone* to cool before removing from the tin. Serve warm or at room temperature.

525G (1LB 1OZ) PLAIN FLOUR

A GOOD PINCH OF SALT

25G (SCANT 1OZ) FRESH YEAST

5 TABLESPOONS OLIVE OIL PLUS EXTRA FOR BRUSHING

For the filling

550G (1¼LB) SPRING ONIONS, CHOPPED

85ML (3FLOZ) EXTRA VIRGIN OLIVE OIL

6 SALTED ANCHOVIES, WELL RINSED AND CHOPPED

200G (7OZ) SMALL BLACK OLIVES, STONED

2 TABLESPOONS SALTED CAPERS, WELL RINSED

500G (1LB 2OZ) PLUM TOMATOES, SKINNED, SEEDED AND DICED

140G (5OZ) SULTANAS, SOAKED IN TEPID WATER FOR 1 MINUTE AND DRAINED

SALT AND FRESHLY GROUND BLACK PEPPER

175G (6OZ) CACIOCAVALLO OR PECORINO, GRATED

CRESCIA DI FORMAGGIO
PLAITED CHEESE BREAD

MAKES **4**

This is a speciality of Iesi, in the Marche, and is served with Parma ham.

Put the flour, grated cheeses, salt and pepper into a large bread crock or bowl. Add the oil and water to the yeast and mix until creamed, then add the yeast mixture to the flour, followed by the beaten eggs. Bring the mixture to a dough and knead by hand for 10 minutes. Leave the dough in a warm place to rise until doubled in size (this may take up to 1 hour).

Knock down the dough and cut into 4 equal pieces. Push one-quarter of the cubed pecorino into each lump of dough. Divide one lump in half and pull each half into an equal length. Plait the 2 pieces together, with the end of the plait slightly folded over, facing upwards, and put into a well-buttered brioche tin. Repeat with the remaining 3 lumps of dough. Cover with a dry, clean tea towel and leave to prove.

Preheat the oven to 180°C/350°F/gas 4. Bake for 35–40 minutes. Turn out and serve hot or cold.

1KG (2¼LB) STRONG PLAIN FLOUR

300G (10½OZ) PECORINO, FRESHLY GRATED

400G (14OZ) PARMESAN, FRESHLY GRATED

20G (¾OZ) SALT

20G (¾OZ) FRESHLY GROUND BLACK OR WHITE PEPPER

200G (7OZ) OLIVE OIL

200G (7OZ) HOT WATER

100G (3½OZ) FRESH YEAST

10 EGGS, BEATEN

300G (10½OZ) PECORINO, CUBED

CRESCENTE

FRIED FLAT BREADS

MAKES **18**

Crescente *are served topped with Parma ham, salami or a fresh (not matured) cheese, such as pecorino, as well as piquant flavourings such as capers and dried chilli flakes. The dough does not have to be used all at once as it will keep for 2 days in the refrigerator. Farina 'O' is an Italian flour available in most Italian delicatessens or in specialist food stores.*

500G (1LB 2OZ) TYPE 'O' FLOUR

1 TEASPOON SALT

A GOOD PINCH OF BICARBONATE OF SODA

300ML (½ PINT) MILK, APPROXIMATELY

EXTRA VIRGIN OLIVE OIL

SEA SALT

Mix the flour, salt, bicarbonate of soda and milk together to make a dough. Wrap the dough in a cloth and leave to rest in the refrigerator for 1 hour.

Break off pieces of dough the size of a golf ball and roll out into discs about 18cm (7in) diameter. Heat a little extra virgin olive oil in a heavy non-stick frying pan. Fry the discs, one at a time, until golden on both sides; they will bubble all over. Change the olive oil in the pan after every 2 or 3 *crescente*. Drain on kitchen paper. Sprinkle with freshly ground sea salt and serve at once.

Panelle

Chickpea fritters

Traditionally in Palermo, where this recipe is a roadside snack speciality, the panelle *are eaten as a filling for* pagnotte, *which are bread rolls covered with sesame seeds. We serve them with warm salads, but they are good just eaten on their own. The* panelle *can be cut in circles, but of course some of the chickpea mixture gets wasted as it cannot be reworked. However, there is nothing to stop one making* maltagliati, *or odd shapes, with the left overs, frying them and sprinkling them on a well-dressed salad in place of croutons. In the Mediterranean basin chickpeas have been used since ancient times.*

1.5 LITRES (2¾ PINTS) COLD
  WATER
SALT
500G (1LB 2OZ) CHICKPEA FLOUR
1 BUNCH OF PARSLEY, FINELY
  CHOPPED
OLIVE OIL FOR DEEP FRYING

Put the cold water in a saucepan with a pinch of salt and slowly add the chickpea flour, stirring constantly with a wooden spoon. Bring to the boil, then reduce the heat and cook, stirring, until the mixture starts to pull away from the sides of the pan. Add the parsley and check the salt. Pour the mixture on to a lightly oiled work surface or plastic board, and spread with a spatula to a layer about 5mm (¼ in) thick. Leave to get cold.

Cut into rectangles, each about 4 x 7cm (10 x 3in). Fry the *panelle*, a few at a time, in hot olive oil until golden brown all over and puffing up. Drain on kitchen paper and serve hot.

150   B R E A D S

Le Cialde Salate

SAVOURY WAFFLES

MAKES **10**

Serve these with grilled pancetta and slices of mushroom that have been sautéed in olive oil with garlic and parsley.

150G (5½OZ) BUTTER

3 EGGS, SEPARATED

6 TABLESPOONS PLAIN FLOUR

SALT

EXTRA VIRGIN OLIVE OIL

Cut the butter into cubes and leave to soften for 1 hour at room temperature. Then work the butter with a wooden spoon until it is a smooth cream. Add the egg yolks to the butter one at a time, beating well with a balloon whisk. Add the flour a little at a time and season with salt. A soft paste should be obtained. Whisk the egg whites until stiff and delicately fold them into the paste using a metal spoon.

Heat a waffle iron on both sides over a moderate heat. Brush the iron with olive oil. Spread a 2mm (⅟₁₆in) thick layer of the paste over the waffle iron. Close the iron, put it back on the heat and cook for 1 minute on each side. Remove the *cialde* with the point of a knife. Serve hot or cold.

Note: Sweet *cialde* can be made by adding 3 tablespoon of caster sugar to the mixture. The sweet *cialde* can be shaped into cones while still hot and then, once cold and set, can be used for serving ice cream.

CIACCI DI RICOTTA

RICOTTA WAFFLES

SERVES 4

Serve these ricotta waffles with salami or prosciutto. Packets of lievito in polvere per salati *(baking powder) are available in Italian delicattesens.*

400G (14OZ) RICOTTA

350ML (12FLOZ) MILK

SALT

250G (9OZ) PLAIN FLOUR

1 PACKET (16G) *LIEVITO IN POLVERE PER SALATI*

OLIVE OIL

Put the ricotta in a bowl. Using a wooden spoon, mix the milk into the ricotta to make a smooth cream. Season with salt. Add the flour and stir until smooth. Finally, add the *lievito in polvere per salati*, still stirring well.

Heat a waffle iron and brush with olive oil. Place a walnut-sized blob of the ricotta mixture on the iron, close it and cook on a moderate heat for a few minutes on each side. The waffles should be amber coloured.

CUCULLI DI FARINA DI CECI

CHICKPEA AND MARJORAM FRITTERS

SERVES 6

Cuculli, a Ligurian speciality, are good served as part of a vegetarian meal, or as a nibble.

400G (14OZ) CHICKPEA FLOUR

30G (1OZ) FRESH YEAST

MARJORAM, FRESH OR DRIED

SUNFLOWER OIL FOR FRYING

SALT

Sift the flour into a bowl. Whisk in enough cold water to obtain a dense, fluid batter. Crumble the yeast into a cup, add a little tepid water and mix together well. Add the yeast to the batter. Cover the bowl and leave the batter to rise for at least 2 hours. Just before frying, add a good pinch of marjoram.

Heat abundant oil in a deep frying pan. When it is hot add small spoonfuls of the batter, a few at a time. Fry until golden and puffed up. Drain on kitchen paper and sprinkle with salt. Serve at once.

THEMED RECIPES

In Italy, a good meal starts with an antipasto, then comes the first course, the primo, *of soup, pasta or rice, and this is followed by the second or main course, the* secondo, *of meat or fish. Vegetables,* contorni, *are always served separately. The meal ends with fruit and cheese, and a dessert if it's a special occasion.*

On the following pages we've suggested some dishes which combine the traditions of Italian cooking with best ingredients from the countryside, coast and sea.

FROM THE COAST	FROM THE FIELDS	FROM THE WILD
Antipasto	*Antipasto*	*Merenda* (Elevenses)
Gamberi Croccanti (Tiger Prawns in a Crisp Pasta Crust)	*Crostini Mediterranei* (Crostini with Aubergine, Tomato and Chilli)	*Ferratelle della Trebbiatura* (Lemon Waffles)
First course	*First course*	*First course*
Spaghetti alle Alghe con Salmone (Spaghetti with Salmon and Samphire)	*Minestra Affumicata* (Smoked Salmon, Leek and Rice Soup) & *Zuppa di Patate con Porri* *e Aglio Selvatico* (Leek and Potato Soup with Wild Garlic)	*Tagliatelle con Ragù di Coniglio* (Tagliatelle with Rabbit Sauce)
Second course		*Second course*
Arrosto di Frutti di Mare *alla Gallese* (Baked Seafood with Laverbread)	*Second course*	*Trote al Forno in Crosta di Speck* (Baked Trout with Speck and Savory) ACCOMPANIMENT: Welsh Bubble and Squeak
	Fettina del Curato (Sirloin Steak with Herb and Anchovy Sauce)	
Dessert		*Dessert*
Trio of Coffee – *Crema Bruciata di Caffè* (Coffee Crème Brûlée), *Panna Cotta al Caffè* (Coffee-flavoured Mascarpone Custard), *Gelato al Caffè* (Coffee Ice Cream)	*Dessert* *Fiori di Zucchini Dolci* (Sweet Fried Courgette Flowers)	Whimberry Sorbet

FROM THE SEA	FROM THE FARMYARD	FROM THE HILLS
Antipasto	*Antipasto*	*Antipasto*
Sgombri alla Pugliese (Mackerel with Mint, Garlic and Chilli)	Lady Llanover's Salt Duck	*Crescente* (Fried Flat Breads)
First course	*First course*	*First course*
Passatelli in Brodo di Pesce (Passatelli in Broth, with Sole, Red Mullet and Scampi)	*Gnocchi di Patate con Sugo di Anitra* (Potato Gnocchi with Duck Sauce)	*Polenta Pasticciata* (Layered Polenta, Mushroom and Fontina Pie)
Second course	*Second course*	*Second course*
Spigola con Carfiofi e Barba di Frate (Seabass with Artichokes and Barba di Frate)	*Maiale ai Capperi* (Pork Medallions with Capers)	*Agnello in Salsa all'Aglio* (Lamb Cutlets with Garlic Sauce) ACCOMPANIMENT: *Porri al Prosciutto Impanati e Fritti* (Wine-Poached Leeks Wrapped in Parma Ham)
Dessert	*Dessert*	*Dessert*
Torta di Formaggio al Limone (Lemon Cheese Cake)	*Gelato di Miele e Armagnac* (Honey and Armagnac Ice Cream)	*Ricotta Fritta* (Fried Ricotta Balls)

INDEX